THE S

# THE SOUL'S TESTING

...............................................

A Dramatic Life Tableau
as Sequel to

"Initiation
.................
The Gate Of Consecration"

*through*

Rudolf Steiner

THE MODERN SPIRIT PRESS
and
TRAFFORD

The stage directions in this drama are from the point of view of the audience.


**The Second Mystery Drama (The Soul's Testing)** is a translation from the German of **Die Prüfung der Seele**. This translation follows the pagination and lineation (with a few minor adjustments necessary for this English printing) of the current German hardback (not paperback) edition **1998**. In German, it is published together with the three other Mystery Dramas as **Vier Mysteriendramen** and may be obtained from Rudolf Steiner Verlag, Dornach, Switzerland, (copyright 1956 by Rudolf Steiner Nachlassverwaltung, Dornach) under the ISBN 3727401400 or ISBN 3727457120 (pocket hardback). This translation has taken into account the first German edition of 1911, the apparent last German edition (1922) during Rudolf Steiner's lifetime, the German editions of 1935, 1948, 1981, as well as 1998.

This drama has been previously translated and published in English under the title **The Soul's Probation**.


Translation copyright: J.C.McCulloch **2004**

No part of this publication may be reproduced, stored in a retrieval system, or transmitted, in any form or by any means, electronic, mechanical, photocopying, recording, or otherwise, without the written prior permission of the translator, except as follows:

The right to use this translation in a theatrical production of this drama (not to reproduce the text for sale or distribution) is hereby made free to everyone.

The right to reproduce and use this translation of 'The Fairy Tale of the Magic Spring' as spoken by **Mrs. Bald** on pages **196-200**, and 'The Fairy Tale of Good and Evil' as spoken by **Mrs. Keen** on page **239**, when accompanied by an acknowledgement of Rudolf Steiner as the author, is hereby made free to everyone.

---

Printed in Victoria, Canada

National Library of Canada Cataloguing in Publication Data

A cataloguing record for this book that includes the U.S. Library of Congress Classification number, the Library of Congress Call number and the Dewey Decimal cataloguing code is available from the National Library of Canada. The complete cataloguing record can be obtained from the National Library's online database at: www.nlc-bnc.ca/amicus/index-e.html

ISBN 1-4120-2365-3

This book was published on-demand in cooperation with Trafford Publishing.
On-demand publishing is a unique process and service of making a book available for retail sale to the public taking advantage of on-demand manufacturing and Internet marketing. On-demand publishing includes promotions, retail sales, manufacturing, order fulfilment, accounting and collecting royalties on behalf of the author.

Suite 6E, 2333 Government St., Victoria, B.C. V8T 4P4, CANADA
Phone      250-383-6864         Toll-free 1-888-232-4444 (Canada & US)
Fax        250-383-6804         E-mail   sales@trafford.com
Web site   www.trafford.com     TRAFFORD PUBLISHING IS A DIVISION OF
                                TRAFFORD HOLDINGS LTD.
Trafford Catalogue #04-0193    www.trafford.com/robots/04-0193.html

## CHARACTERS, FIGURES AND EVENTS

The soul and spiritual experiences of the individuals portrayed in **The Soul's Testing** present a continuation of those put forward in my previously appearing life tableau **INITIATION: The Gate of Consecration**.

**Professor Capesius**
**Benedictus** Hierophant of the Sun Temple
**Philia** ⎫ spiritual beings who mediate ⎫ not allegorical,
**Astrid** ⎬ the connection of the human ⎬ but rather
**Luna** ⎭ soul forces with the cosmos ⎬ as they are
⎬ as realities
**The Other Philia**, the spiritual being who ⎬ for spiritual
hinders the connection of the human soul ⎬ knowledge
forces with the cosmos ⎭

**The Voice of Conscience**
**Maria**
**Johannes Thomasius**
**Doctor Strader** (Doctor of Science/Engineering)
**Felix Bald**
**Mrs. Bald**
**The Double of Johannes Thomasius**

**Lucifer** °
**Ahriman** °

**Peasants**, six men (M) and six women (W)
**Simon the Jew**, previous incarnation of Doctor Strader
**Thomas**, previous incarnation of Johannes Thomasius
**Monk**, previous incarnation of Maria

**Grand Master**, head of a branch of a mystic Brotherhood

Of the same Brotherhood:
**First Preceptor**, previous incarnation of Professor Capesius
**Second Preceptor**
**First Master of Ceremonies**
**Second Master of Ceremonies**

**The Spirit of Benedictus**
**Joseph Keen**, previous incarnation of Felix Bald °
**Mrs. Keen**, previous incarnation of Mrs. Bald
**Bertha**, their daughter, previous incarnation of The Other Maria in **INITIATION**
**Cecilia**, called Cilli, the Keen's foster daughter, previous incarnation of Theodora in **INITIATION**

Hierophants of the Sun Temple:
**Theodosius**
**Romanus**

The events of the sixth, seventh, eighth and ninth scenes are the contents of Capesius's spiritual retrospect into his previous life. Maria and Johannes experience (as the presentation itself shows) this retrospect at the same time; not, however, Strader, whose previous incarnation is seen only by Capesius, Maria and Johannes. The pictures of the retrospect into the Fourteenth Century are to be thought of as the results of imaginative knowledge and are thus placed over against history as an idealized presentation of actual life relationships which are only recognizable in the physical world through their effects. This type of life recapitulation (from the events of the Fourteenth Century into the present) is not to be taken as something generally valid, rather as something that can only happen at a turning point in time. Thus, the conflicts resulting from a previous life, as they are presented here, are also *only* possible for such a period of time as this.

## SCENE ONE

The study and library of Capesius. A brown background. Evening time. Capesius, then spirit figures which are the soul forces; after that Benedictus. This and the following scenes present events lying some years after the time in which **INITIATION: The Gate of Consecration** plays.

CAPESIUS (*reading in a book*):
 "Looking into unrealities with the eye of soul °
 And dreaming in thinking's shadowy images
 According to self-made rules –
 Thus does the erring nature of the individual
 Oft search for the goal and meaning of life.
 Out of soul depths it wants to bring up answers
 To questions aimed at cosmic expanses;
 But with the very first steps,
 Such pondering already dwells in delusion
 And in the end is forced to see its spirit sight
 Impotently feeding only on its self."
 (*Speaking the following.*)
 Thus does the lofty clairvoyant mind of Benedictus,
 In words filled with earnestness, characterize
 The soul path taken by many many people.
 Every word of this strikes me a crushing blow. – –
 They paint a picture, cruelly true,
 Of the path my own life has taken;
 And if at this very moment
 A god were to approach me in anger
 Out of the might of its raging storm,
 Its fearful powers could not
 Torment me more terrifyingly than does the force
 Coming from these destiny-laden words.
 Throughout this long human life,

## The Soul's Testing

I have woven only pictures which are
Displayed shadow-like in a soul dream
That mirrors delusion entangled
Nature and spirit deeds
And wants to solve spectral soul riddles
On the basis of its own dream fabric.
I have restlessly turned my seeking soul
Towards so many goals –
But now I'm forced to clearly recognize,
I myself – I did not live within my soul
When the lines of my thinking, beguiled by delusion,
Wanted to span themselves over into cosmic distances.
- - - - - - - - - -
Thus, what I portrayed in self-pleasing images
Remained only an empty pondering.
Then Thomasius, the young painter,
Entered the course my life had taken; –
Through the use of true soul forces,
He proceeded to the lofty state of mind
That transforms an individual
And out of hidden shafts within the soul
Lets the forces rise up that create
The well-springs of our existence.
What grew up for him from his soul foundations –
That is dormant in every human being,
And because this was revealed to me in him,
I can recognize the greatest sin in life
Is to let spirit treasures go to waste.
- - - - - - - - - -
Thus I now know that I must seek – – –
And not continue to have my doubts.
*Formerly*, my thinking's vain path might have
Led me astray to the false opinion
That our impulse for research is in vain,

*Scene One*

That only renunciation is fitting for all pondering
That strives for the well-springs of life.
- - - - - - - - - -
And if, as something definitely demanded of me
By the powers of human destiny –
If letting my own being sink down
Into an unreal nothingness had been shown me
As the conclusion of all wisdom,
I would have ventured it, undaunted. – – –
To think that way now would be a sacrilege
After I have clearly experienced
I will not be permitted to find peace
Until the spirit treasure within my soul
Has found the light of day.
- - - - - - - - - -
Spirit beings have planted
The fruits of their work in our souls,
And whoever lets the spirit seeds decay,
Uncared for, destroys the work of the gods.
Thus I can now recognize life's highest duty; –
Yet when I want to venture but one step
Into that realm I'm not permitted to avoid,
I feel the forces forsaking me
By which I, in a thinking full of pride,
Wanted to indicate the goals of life
In the wide world and in the stream of time.
At one point, I believed I could squeeze
Out of my brain with ease
The thoughts to grasp realities;
But now that I want to grasp
The well-spring of life in the light of truth,
My thinking's instrument seems dull –
And powerlessly I agonize
To form clear images of thought

## The Soul's Testing

From Benedictus's earnest words,
Which are supposed to show me spirit pathways:
*(Again reading the following.)*
"Penetrate calmly into your soul's depths,
And let fortitude be your guide.
As you sink into yourself,
Shed your earlier forms of thinking
In order to guide you to yourself.
Deadening all your own light,
Spirit brightness appears."
*(Again speaking the following.)*
It's as if my very breath were to fail me
When I strive to make sense out of words like these,
And before I can feel what I'm to think,
Anxiety and fright grip my soul.
I'm forced to feel as if everything
Surrounding me in life up till now
Could fall apart and transform me
Into a nothingness within its ruins.
Oh, a hundred times I've read
The words that follow next; – – –
With each and every time, the darkness
Surrounding me has only grown darker.
*(Again reading.)*
"In your thinking are living cosmic thoughts,
In your feelings are weaving cosmic forces,
In your willing are working cosmic beings.
Lose yourself in cosmic thoughts,
Experience yourself through cosmic forces,
Create yourself from beings of will.
Do not end up in cosmic distances
Through the dreamy play of thinking; – – –
Begin in the wide spirit widths
And end up in your own soul depths –

*Scene One*

Recognizing yourself in you,
You come upon divine goals."
*(Made powerless by a vision, sinking into himself. Then coming to himself, speaking the following.)*
What was this?
*(Three figures, as soul forces, hover around him.)*

LUNA:

    For lofty spirit flight,
    You do not lack the strength;
    That is well grounded
    In the human will,
    That is well hardened
    By hope's certainty,
    That is well tempered
    By sight of distant future.
    You only lack the courage
    To pour into your willing
    New confidence in life. – – –
    To venture the wide unknown,
    Simply embolden yourself!

ASTRID:

    Out of the sun's joyful light
    From cosmic distances –
    Out of the magical cosmic power
    From the starry expanses –
    Out of the spirit's lofty force
    From the blue ether of heaven –
    Aspire to soul power
    And direct its rays
    To the heart's foundations,
    Then will knowledge, warming,
    Create itself in you.

## The Soul's Testing

**THE OTHER PHILIA:**
    They're deceiving you,
    Those evil sisters.
    They want to spin round you
    A phantasmagorical game of life. °
    The vain illusion of gifts
    They reach out to you
    Will dissolve away
    When you try to maintain it
    With your human strength.
    They'll lead you on
    To worlds of gods
    And will destroy you
    If you defiantly venture
    To seek your being
    In their realm.

**CAPESIUS:**
    It was quite clear – – –
    Beings were speaking here – –
    And yet, it's certain – –
    Nobody outside of myself
    Is at this place – – – –
    - - - - - - - - - -
    So have I only spoken to my self? – – –
    That too is impossible;
    For I could never think up
    What I believe I heard – –
    - - - - - - - - - -
    Am I still now who I was before this?
    *(From his gestures is to be noticed that he feels himself unable to answer "Yes".)*
    Oh – I am – I am not – °
    - - - - - - - - - -

## Scene One

**A SPIRIT VOICE, SPIRITUAL CONSCIENCE:**
Your thoughts are now climbing
Into the depths of your being.
What as soul here encases you,
What as spirit's spellbound in you,
Wafts away into cosmic foundations;
> From whose bounty
> Human beings, drinking,
> Live within thinking;
> From whose bounty
> Human beings, living,
> Weave in the shining. °

**CAPESIUS:**
Too much .... too much – –
Where is Capesius?
I plead with you,
You unknown Powers,
Where is ..... Capesius?
Where am I myself?
*(He sinks brooding into himself once again.)*

**BENEDICTUS** *(Enters. At first Capesius does not notice him. Benedictus touches him on the shoulder.):*
Information has reached me
You are demanding to speak with me,
So I have sought you out in your own home.

**CAPESIUS:**
It's so good of you
To fulfill my wish,
But you could hardly find me
In a worse situation.

## The Soul's Testing

- - - - - - - - - -
And that after such agony of soul
As I've just now been racked by,
I'm not at this very moment
Lying paralyzed on the floor before you,
I owe solely to that mild glance
That met mine when your hand
So gently woke me from those terrifying dreams.

**BENEDICTUS:**
From me is not hidden that I find you
In the midst of a struggle for existence. °
Already long ago I knew
We would have to meet in this way.
If we are to thoroughly understand one another,
Accustom yourself to changing
The sense of a good many words,
And then don't be surprised if your suffering
Must change its name in my language.
- - - - - - - - - -
I find you in good fortune.

**CAPESIUS:**
Now you increase still more the anguish
That threw me into those dark regions.
A moment ago, I felt as if my own self
Had fled away into cosmic depths,
And strange beings were speaking in this room
Through members of my self. –
That I was allowed to experience
Such a phantasmagorical game of spirits as delusion,
And that that deception of my soul was painful,
That alone held me upright.
Oh, don't rob me of the support of such feelings! –

## Scene One

Don't call good fortune what was feverish delusion–
If I am not to become completely lost.

**BENEDICTUS:**
Human beings can only lose
What separates them from the world being,
And if at first they seem to lose
What they've misused for unreal service
Within the dreamy moods of thinking,
Then they should seek
For what has separated from them.
They will find it once again
And first then consecrate it
In the right way to our human work.
To console you at this particular time
Would be a pedantic play on words.

**CAPESIUS:**
No – teachings that satisfy reason alone
Are quite truly not to be found with you.
With difficulty I've had to learn that.
Like deeds that lead to the heights
And also plunge into the depths of the abyss,
Just so, fiery life and deathly cold stream
Powerfully into human souls through your discourses.
They work like a wink of destiny
And also like one of life's love storms.
I had thought, and searched,
Before I met you; – –
The spirit's creating forces
And its work of destroying,
These I first learned to know
After I began following your footsteps.
- - - - - - - - - -

## The Soul's Testing

What your words brought about in my soul,
You discovered just now
As you entered my study.
I have often been tormented
When reading in your book of life,
But today, due to those
Destiny-laden words in the book,
The measure of my torment came full,
And my soul distress overflowed.
Understanding of the discourse
Remained closed to my soul,
Yet like a life-giving elixir
The words poured themselves into my heart
And created such magical worlds
That my senses' clarity faded away.
I saw phantom beings fluttering round me.
I could hear significant, dark words
Sounding out of a crazed, pathological soul.
I know you don't want to entrust to your writings
Everything you keep guarded for human souls,
And that you direct many a solution
Of a riddle to an individual according to need,
So don't begrudge me what I need,
For I have to know,
What robbed me of my sense and reason
And surrounded me with dizzying, magical spells.

**BENEDICTUS:**

My words not only want to say
What they convey as coverings for concepts;
They direct a soul's forces
To spirit realities;
Their sense is first reached
When they release vision in the soul

## Scene One

That has given itself up to their force.
They don't arise out of my research.
They are entrusted to me by the Spirits
Who keep informed about the signs
By which World Karma is revealed.
The peculiar nature of these words is
To guide one to the well-springs of knowledge,
Yet it must remain for each individual
Who listens to them within their own true being
To drink the spirit elixir from its springs;
And it's not contrary to the purpose of my words
That they bear you away into worlds
Which seem spectral to you.
You have now entered a realm
That must remain delusion for you
If you lose your self within it,
But will quite certainly open for your soul
The first gate to complete wisdom,
When you can maintain your self within it.

**CAPESIUS:**
And how can I maintain my self within it?

**BENEDICTUS:**
The solution to that riddle will come
When with an awake eye of soul
You place yourself before the many
Wondrous things soon to come your way.
I see you called to a testing
By the spirit Rulers and the Powers of Destiny.
*(Goes out.)*

**CAPESIUS:**
True, I can't understand the meaning of his words,

*The Soul's Testing*

Yet I feel them working within my being.
He has shown me a goal: – –
I must respond to this sign of destiny.
He didn't demand striving in thoughts;
He wants that through searching
I guide my steps to spirit realities.
- - - - - - - - - -
I don't know the beings he has sent,
Yet what he does compels trust;
He did bring me back to my self.
So for the time being then,
Let that magical being that terrified me
Still remain unclarified;
I want to place myself with open mind over against
The things he has prophetically made known. °

(Curtain, while Capesius still remains standing.)

## SCENE TWO

A meditation room with a violet background. A serious, but not gloomy mood. Benedictus, Maria, then spirit figures representing the soul forces.

**MARIA:**
>Difficult soul battles are urging me
>To now listen to my guide's wise advice. °
>A dark premonition has arisen in my heart,
>And I'm not capable
>Of opposing the thoughts
>Ever and again storming in upon me.
>They strike into the deepest core of my being;
>They want to impose a command on me
>It would seem like a sacrilege to obey.
>The Rulers of Deception must be bewitching me; – –
>I beseech you – help me – –
>So I can banish them.

**BENEDICTUS:**
>There should never be a time you lack
>What you wish to have from me. °

**MARIA:**
>I know how closely bound to my soul
>Are the ways of Johannes's life.
>A difficult path of destiny has united us,
>And in higher spirit worlds
>The divine will has consecrated our union.
>All this stands quite clearly before me
>As the only possible picture of reality;
>And yet – right away I'm seized with horror °
>When I'm supposed to set my lips

## The Soul's Testing

To these sacrilegious words, –
And yet – out of my own soul depths
I hear them speaking to me quite clearly
And always repeating themselves anew
When I believe them overcome,
"You must separate Johannes from yourself;
You may not hold him at your side
If you wish to avoid harm to his soul.
He must travel alone the road
That will lead him to his own goals."
I know if you were to speak but one word
This delusory fabrication would flee my soul.

**BENEDICTUS:**
    Maria, for you a noble suffering has here
    Let the truth appear as deceptive image.

**MARIA:**
    It could be – the truth – – – –
    But no! – even between my guide's words
    And my hearing, this delusion inserts itself.
    Oh, speak a second time.

**BENEDICTUS:**
    You have correctly understood me. –
    Your love is of a noble kind,
    And Johannes has been closely bound to you;
    Nevertheless love must not forget
    She is sister to wisdom.
    For the good of Johannes,
    He has been united with you through long ages,
    But now his soul's further road demands
    He himself seek his own goals in freedom.
    The will of destiny does not speak

## Scene Two

Of external separation for this friendship,
But it very strictly demands Johannes's
Independent deeds within the realm of the spirit.

**MARIA:**
  Still again I hear delusion!
  Then simply let *me* speak further;
  You must understand me,
  For no deceptive image would dare
  To change my words before your ear.
  It would be easy to banish all doubt
  If only the tangled course of my own earthly life
  Wished to hold Johannes's soul to that of mine,
  But the consecration that eternally binds
  Soul to soul was bestowed upon our union,
  And spirit Rulers spoke with blessings
  The words banishing all doubt,
  "He has achieved the truth for himself
  Within the realm of eternity
  Because he was already bound to you
  In the sense world in the very depths of existence."
  How can I understand this revelation
  If now the opposite is to be taken as the truth?

**BENEDICTUS:**
  You must learn how very much can still be lacking
  Towards full maturity even for one who has already
  Been permitted to experience many revelations.
  The pathways to the higher truth are confusing; —
  Those alone are capable of orienting themselves
  Who can walk through the labyrinths with patience.
  When a picture of the Land of Spirits
  Came before your eyes of soul,
  You were able to behold, to begin with,

## The Soul's Testing

A part of reality in that realm of exalted light;
That picture is not yet the full reality.
Johannes's soul and that of yours
Are joined together by earthly bonds of such a kind
That to each one may be allotted the finding
Of their way into the domain of the spirit
By means of forces they owe the other.
Until now, however, nothing has revealed
*Whether you both have fulfilled all the requirements.*
You have been permitted to behold in pictures
What is allotted to you both for the future
When you are able to pass the full testing.
That the fruits of your striving
Are shown to you now, does not prove
You have reached the end of your striving.
You both have beheld a *picture* – –
But only your wills alone
Can change that picture into a reality.

**MARIA:**

Though your words strike me like the most
Intense pain after a long sense of well-being,
Still, I have learned well enough
To submit myself to the light of wisdom
When it is shown to be effective by its inner force,
And what was dark for my heart until now
Already begins to clear;
But if in a most wonderful experience of happiness,
A facade of errors overpoweringly
Gives itself out to common sense as the truth,
Then soul darkness will be hard to banish.
I need still more than you've given up till now if
I'm to be able to really follow your words as well.
You guided my self into those soul foundations

*Scene Two*

Where light was granted me
So that I was then permitted to survey
The earthy lives allotted me in long past ages.
I was allowed to experience how my soul
And that of my friend had found each other.
That in those ancient times I guided
Johannes's soul to true spirit words,
I was permitted to see as the seed kernel
That, ripenning, brought us this fruit:
A friendship deemed to be ripe for all eternity.

**BENEDICTUS:**
>You were recognized as worthy
>To penetrate to those earthly paths
>Allotted you
>In days long past,
>But when you turn your spirit eye backwards,
>You should not forget to search out
>Whether you are also so certain
>None of your life paths are hidden from you.

**MARIA** *(after a pause indicating deep self-reflection)*:
>Oh, how could I have been so blinded!
>The blissfulness I experienced
>When permitted to view a part of earlier times
>Has in vain delusion long let me forget
>How much I still lack,
>And only now am I able to intuit
>I must look into the darknesses
>If I want to discover the pathway leading
>From life in the present into those times
>When the soul of my friend
>Turned itself towards mine.
>To you, my guide, I give my pledge

## The Soul's Testing

To tame my soul's presumption! – –
Only now do I recognize how the vanity
Of knowing can lead the soul astray
So that instead of drawing strength
From the spiritual possessions given it,
It only wants to use those gifts
To wantonly reflect itself.
By means of my heart's warning call,
Which your words lend strength to,
I now know how very far away
From even my nearest goal
I still must feel.
Not too hastily in future will I interpret
What I learn from the Spiritland.
I shall treasure it as a force
To fashion my soul –
And not as a directive
Saving me the trouble of recognizing
The goals of my deeds within life itself.
Had I earlier followed
Those words demanding circumspection,
It wouldn't have remained obscured
That my friend's richly endowed soul
Can only unfold itself freely
When it itself seeks ways
Not mapped out for it by me;
And in that I recognize this now,
I shall win the strength
To do what love and duty demand.
Yet at this moment I feel more
Than I have ever felt before
That I stand before a difficult soul testing.
When in other cases, people tear from their heart
What of the one lives in the other,

## Scene Two

Then love is changed into its opposite;
They themselves change the bonds that bind them,
Yet their drive and passion give them strength.
I, however, by my own free will, am to cancel out
The effects that I saw brought about
By my own soul life on my friend's deeds,
And yet my love must remain unchanged.

**BENEDICTUS:**

You will follow this path in the right sense
If you are willing to recognize
What the most valuable part of that love was.
For when you know which force
Is directing you unconsciously in your soul,
Then you will find the power
To do what duty must demand of you.

**MARIA:**

In speaking of this, you have already given
My soul the help it needs so much at this time.
To the very depths of my being
I must put this earnest question, "What is driving
Me on with such great power in this love?"
I see my soul's own life effectively working within
My friend's being and in his artistic creating.
Thus I seek after a satisfaction
I then feel about my own self
And may live in the delusion I am selfless;
But the fact has remained concealed from me
That in my friend I only mirror my *self*.
It was the dragon of self-seeking °
That deceptively masked
What truly drove me on.
I am now forced to recognize that

Self-seeking transforms itself a hundredfold,
And if one considers it as conquered,
It simply arises with still greater force
Out of the wreckage of its rule
And then gains the additional strength
To deceptively reveal delusion as the truth.
*(Maria falls into deep pondering. Exit Benedictus.)*

- - - - - - - - - -

*(The three figures of the soul forces appear.)*

**MARIA:**

You, my sisters, who I find
In the depths of my being
When my soul expands itself
And conducts its self
Into cosmic distances,
Release the forces of seership
From the etheric heights
And lead them onto earthly paths,
So I may discover my self
Within time's existence
And give myself the direction
From ancient modes of life
To new circuits of my will.

- - - - - - - - - -

**PHILIA:**

From the heart's depths
I shall fill myself
With striving soul light,
From spirit impulses
I shall breath into myself
Enlivening will power,
So that you, beloved sister,

May feel the light
Within your ancient life circuits.
- - - - - - - - - -

ASTRID:
    I shall weave together
    A self-experiencing nature
    With devotedly loving will;
    I shall release
    Sprouting will powers
    From the chains of desire,
    And transform laming longing
    Into receptive spirit feelings,
    So that you, beloved sister,
    May discover your self
    On distant earthly pathways.
- - - - - - - - - -

LUNA:
    I shall call forth renouncing heart powers
    And shall consolidate supporting soul peace.
    They will wed themselves together
    And out of the soul's foundations
    Raise up strengthening spirit illumination;
    They will interpenetrate each other
    And compel far off earthly times
    To a listening spirit ear,
    So that you, beloved sister,
    May find the traces of your life
    In time's wide existence.
- - - - - - - - - -

MARIA (*after a pause*):
    If I can tear myself away

*The Soul's Testing*

---

From bewildering self-esteem
And am allowed to give myself to you
So you can reflect my soul existence
From cosmic distances,
I'll be capable of freeing myself
From the circuit of this life
And be able to discover myself
In other modes of existence.
*(Longer pause, then the following.)*

MARIA:
In you, my sisters, I behold those spirit beings
Which bring souls to life out of the whole universe.
The forces germinating in eternity you can
Bring to maturity in the human being itself.
Through the gates of my soul I was often
Permitted to find the way to your realms
And with my eyes of soul look upon
The primordial forms of earth existence.
Now I am in need of your help
As I am obliged to find the way
From my present earthly voyage
Into long past days of humanity.
Release my soul existence
From its self-esteem in this life in time;
Disclose to me the circuit of my duties
From the course my lives took in earlier ages.

- - - - - - - - - - -

A SPIRIT VOICE, SPIRITUAL CONSCIENCE:
Her thoughts are now seeking
In the traces of time,
What as debt remains to her,
What as duty is given her,

*Scene Two*

May emerge from her soul foundation,
Out of whose depths
Human beings, dreaming,
Guide their lives;
Into whose depths
Human beings, erring.
Lose their selves.

(The curtain falls while everyone is still on the stage.)

## SCENE THREE

A room with a rose-red background; congenial atmosphere. Johannes before an easel; later Maria enters; then spirit figures as the soul forces.

**JOHANNES:**
    The last time she looked at it,
    Maria remained silent before my picture. –
    Previously though, she always gave
    From the rich treasure of her wisdom
    What could help my work's progress.
    Just as little as I trust myself
    To form a judgement on my own
    About whether I fulfil with my art
    What our spiritual stream demands,
    Just so much do I trust her, –
    And ever and again I hear in my mind
    Those strength bestowing words that brought joy
    As I ventured forth on this painting.
    "On this pathway," she said,
    "You can undertake the bold venture
    Of revealing to sense appearance
    What the soul beholds only in spirit.
    How forms, being similar to thoughts,
    Compel matter,
    How colors, related to feelings,
    Warm our life force,
    These will not remain hidden from you.
    Thus you will be allowed to portray
    The higher realms, too, with your abilities."
    Sensing the strength in these words,
    I diffidently gave myself up to the belief
    I was drawing nearer to the goal

## Scene Three

Benedictus had indicated to me.
Often I sat before this painting disheartened,
Much of the time it really seemed presumptuous,
At other moments, it appeared simply impossible
To represent in colors and in forms
What my soul is now permitted to behold.
How one can reveal a weaving spirit existence
Disclosing itself only to the clairvoyant eye
When the whole of sense appearance is removed,
But now with means still belonging
To the realm of the senses,
This I asked my self time and again.
Yet when I do banish my own individuality
And, following the sense of our spirit teachings,
Am allowed to feel myself being borne away in
Blessedness to the Creating Powers of the cosmos,
A faith awakens in me
In an art as mystically true
As our spirit searching is.
I've learned to live with the light
And recognize the deeds of the light in the colors
Just as true students of genuine mysticism behold
The spirit's deeds and the soul's existence
Within the realm of colorless and formless life.
With trust in such a spirit light,
I have won the ability
To feel with the flooding sea of light,
To live with the streaming glow of colors,
Intuiting ruling spirit Powers
Within the matter-emptied weaving of light,
Within the spirit-filled life of colors.
(*Maria enters, without being noticed by Johannes*)
- - - - - - - - - -
And when my courage fails me,

## The Soul's Testing

I think of your person, noble friend. –
My desire to create
Is warmed in your soul fire;
My powers of faith
Are awakened in your spirit light.
*(He sees Maria.)*
Oh – you are here, – – – – –
I await your person impatiently
And yet could overlook your coming!

**MARIA:**
It really does fill me with delight
To see my friend so absorbed in his work
He can forget even his dear friend.

**JOHANNES:**
Oh, don't say such things, –
You know I can create nothing
Not blessed by you.
There is no work of mine
That doesn't owe its origins to you.
You have purified me in the fire of love so that
Through my art I'm now capable of portraying what
Is revealed to you within beauty's brilliance, what
Rays out, clarifying existence and warming beings,
And in raying out, reveals the Spiritland.
I have to sense the stream of my creating flowing
Into my soul from that well-spring in yours,
Then I can feel the wings that lift me up
To those far from earth, spirit-filled heights. –
I love what lives within your soul
And can lovingly bestow picture form upon it.
For the artist, only love can bring to birth
The forces that live on productively in his works;

## Scene Three

And if as an artist I'm to carry pictures
From spirit expanses into the world of the senses,
Then the cosmic spirit must appear through me
And my own being must simply be its instrument.
I must be able to burst the chains of self-seeking
So I wouldn't even want to artistically portray
The delusory figures of my own capriciousness
Instead of the worlds of the spirits.

----------

MARIA:
And if, instead of through my soul vision, you
Had to get your work's original image from yourself,
Then the nature of beauty could work in a more
Unified way out of *one* person's soul foundations.

----------

JOHANNES:
I'd simply be chasing vain wisps of thought
If I were to brood about which seems better:
To create your spirit vision in a physical form,
Or to seek the origin of the image within my self.
I know I couldn't find it that way.

----------

I can sink myself into my soul foundations
And blessedly find myself in spirit worlds;
I can lose myself in the realm of the senses
And with my eye follow the miracles of color
Which allow me to behold acts of creation.
When I am quite alone with my soul,
What I can experience in myself leads an existence
That simply doesn't drive me to create; yet when
I'm permitted to follow you into cosmic heights
And in blessedness, warmly experience from you what

## The Soul's Testing

You have already looked on there within the spirit,
Then I sense a fire in that spirit vision that
Continues burning within my self, and flaming up,
Ignites forces in me that impel me to create.

- - - - - - - - - -

If I wanted to make known to people in words
What I can recognize in the higher worlds,
I'd be allowed to raise myself with my own soul
Into spheres where spirit speaks to spirit.
As artist, I have to find the fire that works
By raying forth out of the work into the heart,
And my soul can only give to the picture what
Magically streams a burning spirit glow to the heart
If it can itself first drink that spirit revelation
From out of the depths of *your* heart.

- - - - - - - - - -

How primordial forces densify themselves into longing,
And Creating Powers flash forth spiritizing and,
Already feeling the human being needs to exist,
Create themselves as gods at time's beginning,
All this the soul of my friend has often let me
Grasp in an invisible way with exalted words.
Sensing how colors harbor a longing to behold
Themselves spiritually transfigured within souls,
I attempted to densify the invisible
Within the delicate etheric red of the spirit world.
Thus does my friend's soul speak to human hearts
From out of my pictures as if it were my own.

MARIA:
> Consider, Johannes, that the One soul, separated °
> From others, must have been unfolding its self as
> Its own individuality since the world's beginning.
> Love should bind separate individuals,

*Scene Three*

But not want to kill their own particular natures.
For us the point in time has come
When we must put our souls to the test
Of how they are to direct our next steps
On the spirit pathway for the benefit of each of us.
- - - - - - - - - -
*(Exit.)*

**JOHANNES:**
What did my friend say?
Her words sounded so incomprehensible!
I have to follow you, Maria! – – –
*(The three figures of the soul forces appear.)*

**LUNA:**
You cannot find your self
In the reflected image of another soul.
The force of your own being
Must put down roots in cosmic ground
If it wants to plant, in the right sense,
The beauty from spirit heights
Into the earth's depths.
Embolden yourself for your own existence
So you can offer yourself to cosmic Powers
As a strong soul form.
- - - - - - - - - -

**ASTRID:**
You should not wish to lose yourself
Along your cosmic pathways.
Individuals who want to rob themselves of their
Own existence do not penetrate to sun distances.
So prepare yourself
To press on through earthly love

Into the deep foundations of the heart
Where cosmic love may ripen.

- - - - - - - - - -

**THE OTHER PHILIA:**
Oh, don't listen to those sisters.
They'll lead you on to cosmic expanses
And rob you of the earth's nearness. —
They do not see how earthly love
Bears the traits of cosmic love.
Their natures rule in coldness,
Their forces flee from warmth,
And they wish to lure individuals
Out of their own soul depths
Into those cold, higher worlds.

(Curtain, while Johannes, The Other Philia, Astrid, and Luna still remain standing.)

## SCENE FOUR

The same room as in the first scene. Capesius and Strader.

CAPESIUS (*to Strader as he is entering*):
    With what joy do I greet my old friend
    Who so valiantly withstood me
    In many a hot battle of words.
    You haven't let yourself be seen
    In my house for quite a while. -
    Earlier though, you used to visit it gladly enough.

STRADER:
    I haven't had the time.
    My life has greatly changed.
    I torment my brain no longer
    With hopeless wisps of thought.
    I've devoted all the learning I myself have gained
    To the service of real work
    That can endow life with benefits.

CAPESIUS:
    So have you then abandoned the path of research?

STRADER:
    One could also say,
    I have been abandoned by it.

CAPESIUS:
    And to what goal have you now turned yourself?

STRADER:
    Life is not suited
    To show the individual goals

## The Soul's Testing

He can see the end of in a clear light.
It's only a drive mechanism
That draws us into its running gears – –
And throws us out into darkness, weary,
When the measure of our forces is spent.

**CAPESIUS:**
I first got to know you when with lofty courage
You were boldly venturing the riddles of existence.
I then also experienced
How you saw already won treasures of knowledge
Sink into the foundationless void,
And how your soul, deeply shaken, drank the
Bitter cup of a researcher's disappointed dreams;
But the thought never crossed my mind
You could tear out of your heart
The impulse so completely filling you then.

**STRADER:**
Can you still recall the day
When a seeress, through the truth of her words,
Clearly proved to me the error of my own path?
I couldn't do anything else but admit to myself
That all the work of our thinking
Cannot find the real source of life anywhere.
For all thinking must definitely be in error
If the light of highest wisdom
Could disclose itself to the soul force
That woman called her own.
In any case, strict science certainly strives
In vain for such a revelation.
Had the matter just rested there,
At that *one* setback to my researcher's delusions,
I believe I might have been capable

## Scene Four

Of starting again from the beginning,
And of linking up my own path
With those other paths;
But when I was forced to see
How a quite peculiar type of thinking,
Which appeared to me as simply sheer madness,
Transformed powerlessness into a creative force,
All hope left me.
- - - - - - - - - -
Do you recall that young painter
Whom we met together
On those dubious spirit pathways? – –
After such strokes of destiny as those,
I lived through many weeks
With a dulled mind, close to madness;
And as nature brought me back to my senses again,
It was also settled for me, rock solid,
To avoid all further seeking.
I needed a long time
To become completely well again.
I lived through it with little joy.
I trained in such things
As led me to life's practical experiences.
So now I'm in charge of a workshop
Where screws are turned;
Yet I have this work to thank
That for many hours I'm able to forget
How full of agony my meaningless struggling was.

**CAPESIUS**:

I must confess, I can hardly
Find my former friend again
In the one who presents himself to me today. – –
Apart from such times you've spoken of,

## The Soul's Testing

Don't you also experience moments
When the old storms are renewed
That push you out of this dulled-down life?

**STRADER:**
I have not been spared those hours
In which powerlessness simply wants to battle
With powerlessness within my soul,
But my destiny has not willed
That new rays of hope
For this completely forlorn life
Should penetrate into my heart.
I wish now to achieve renunciation for myself.
The strength this is demanding of me
May bring me the abilities
To transform the researcher's path into another,
- - - - - - - - - - -
When this earthly way is taken again.

**CAPESIUS:**
You speak, – or have I rightly heard,
Of the repetition of your earthly life.
So have you then truly
Won this difficult, destiny-laden truth
On those roads to the spirit
You still want to hold as dubious
Even today?

**STRADER:**
You yourself have there discovered
The third thing that determined me
To begin a new life.
On my sick-bed, I undertook
For the last time to again survey

## Scene Four

The extent of knowledge I had won for myself.
I did that before I turned to other goals;
And a hundred times I asked myself,
"As we can already now survey it,
What can this knowledge of nature teach us?"
– – – There is no way around it: – – –
A thinking that is not to break with everything
The researcher's diligence has learned
In the course of long ages, can and
Must not deny the repetition of earthly lives.

**CAPESIUS:**

A very great deal of suffering would have been
Spared me by way of such an experience.
Throughout many a night
I have passed in sleeplessness,
I longed for thoughts of this sort
To bring me deliverance.

**STRADER:**

Yet this spirit flash
Actually robbed me of my last forces.
I have always felt my soul's strongest impulse
Was to test on life
What thinking gave me as the truth.
In those difficult days, an incident then chose
To prove on my own existence how cruel
This truth with its difficult consequences is.
For it lets the joys and sorrows of life
Appear as the consequences of our own nature,
And this is often very hard to bear.

**CAPESIUS:**

This experience would seem impossible –

## The Soul's Testing

    One that could outshine a truth
    We are ever continually seeking
    And that gives our spirit certainty.

STRADER:
    It may be so for you,
    But I have had to experience otherwise.
    The peculiar course of my life is known to you –
    What once seemed but an accident
    Crossing my parent's intentions. –
    They had wanted to make me into a monk.
    They had often said to me
    They would have to see the heresy of their son
    As the greatest sorrow of their life.
    I took all that in – –
    And a lot more besides,
    Just as one takes in life
    When one makes birth and death
    The boundaries of this earthly pilgrimage;
    And my later life as well,
    With all its crushed hopes,
    Placed itself before me as a picture
    That could only be clarified through itself.
    Oh, would that that day had never come
    That brought me to another view.
    For know, I have not confided to you everything
    Destiny has laid upon me.
    I am not the child of those people
    Who wanted to make me into a monk.
    They had adopted me
    When I was just a few days old.
    My real origins are unknown to me.
    Thus I was already a stranger in my parents' house,
    And I have remained estranged from everything

## Scene Four

I have experienced around me in later years;
And now my thinking obliges me
To turn my gaze to ancient times
When I denied my self the world.
Thought on thought string themselves together;
Whoever is destined to be a stranger to this world
Has already chosen their own destiny
Before they could even will it in thought,
Even before their consciousness dawned;
And as I've remained like this since then,
Just as I was at my beginning,
Every doubt must therefore vanish
That in a dulled-down state, I succumb to Powers
That spin my threads of destiny
And don't wish to reveal themselves to me.
What is still lacking to cruelly prove
How thick the veils are
Cloaking my own existence from myself!
So now judge, oh, without false scholarly obsession,
Whether my new truth has brought me light?
It has, however, given me the certainty
That I must remain in uncertainty.
It has so laid my destiny before me
That, half filled with pain
And half scornfully like itself,
I have paid it back in the same coin.
Quite terrifyingly it came to me:
Tormented throughout with bitter scornful feelings,
I would have to place myself over against life, and
Laughing at destiny's whole phantasmagorical game,
Give myself up to the darkness.
I could still think only one more thing –
Take me in totally you running gears of life,
I don't want to know how you drive it on.

CAPESIUS:
> The man I used to know in you,
> He could not for long remain in such a
> Barrenness of knowledge even if he wanted to.
> Before my eyes the days already appear
> In which we will find each other otherwise.

(Curtain falls while the two men are still standing opposite each other.)

## SCENE FIVE

A countryside in which the solitary house of the Bald's is situated. Evening time. Mrs. Bald, Capesius, then Felix Bald; later Johannes and his Double, afterwards Lucifer and Ahriman.

**CAPESIUS** (*arriving and approaching a bench on which Mrs. Bald is sitting in front of the Bald's house*):
>You'll surely allow an old friend
>To while away a bit of time with you?
>More now than ever before he's in need
>Of what he's so often found in your house.

**MRS. BALD:**
>Even as I saw you coming in the distance
>Your weary footsteps told me of you,
>And as you drew nearer, your eyes also said
>Troubles dwell within your soul today.

**CAPESIUS:**
>To bring much cheerfulness into your home
>Was not given me even in former times;
>Yet today I ask for special forbearance
>If I break into this home of peace
>With a heart lacking in peace.

**MRS. BALD:**
>You were always so very gladly seen here before
>When hardly any one else
>Came near this house. -
>In spite of much that has come between us,
>You have still remained our friend,
>Even when quite a few are now eagerly seeking out
>This site so distant from the world.

## The Soul's Testing

CAPESIUS:

    So it's true what I've heard,
    That your dear Felix,
    Who previously was so closed off,
    Has become a man much sought-after
    In these days?

MRS. BALD:

    Ah yah, my good Felix
    Once closed us off from the whole world, – –
    And now he has to give answer to so many people.
    This new life appears to him as his duty.
    In former times, what the woods
    And rocky cliffs revealed about
    Spirit deeds and the Rulers of Nature,
    He would entrust only to his own inner soul.
    It also didn't seem worth knowing to anyone then.
    - - - - - - - - - -
    But how the times have changed!
    Quite a few people are now listening
    Right greedily to the knowledge
    Felix is able to reveal to them
    And that they previously found simply foolish;
    And when my dear good man
    *(Felix Bald comes out of the house.)*
    Often has to relate things for hours on end,
    Then I long for the olden days
    When Felix would so earnestly point out
    How only within a still heart
    Should the soul bear the spirit gifts
    Bestowed on her in grace
    From the realms of the gods –
    And whoever revealed the lofty spirit words

*Scene Five*

> To ears opened only to the sense world,
> They would be a traitor to them.

**FELIX BALD:**
> Felicia can only reconcile herself with difficulty
> To our completely changed way of life;
> She complained about the old solitude
> And doesn't complain any the less now
> When we have only a few hours left
> For our selves on some days.

**CAPESIUS:**
> And what has induced you
> To hospitably open your house to people,
> When previously it was so closed off.

**FELIX BALD:**
> Obediently I followed the spirit guidance
> That speaks within my heart
> When it commanded me to remain silent,
> And now when it bids me speak,
> I wish to be equally faithful to it.
> The nature of humanity is changing
> With the course of the earth's existence.
> We stand at a turning point in time.
> A part of spiritual knowledge
> Must now be disclosed to all human beings
> Who want to open their heart and feelings to it. – –
> I know how little my style fits in with
> The forms that people accept nowadays.
> In order to speak of what lives within the mind, °
> They prescribe the strictest logic
> And thought construction,
> And these are denied to be in my talks.

## The Soul's Testing

They say that for that true science
Which should be set only on firm supports,
My person may well be taken as an example of how
Human souls may dream when they seek wisdom on
Their own paths estranged from science and learning;
Yet many hold it may be worthwhile,
How through the confusion of my words
Something can be discovered now and again
Which lets itself be grasped by reason.
I am a man for whom must flow
Into his heart without training
Whatever wants to reveal itself to him.
I do not know a knowing without words. –
When I commune with the depths of my heart
And also when I listen in on nature,
Then there lives in me a knowing
That doesn't need to first seek for words; – – –
Its language is as much bound up with it as is
The physical form with the earthly human being. –
A way of knowing that reveals itself to us
From spirit worlds in this manner
May also help people who don't understand it.
Therefore, everyone who wishes
To hear what I have to say
Must be allowed to come to me.
I know full well how many are only led on
By curiosity and other still less good reasons;
Yet even if the souls of such people
Are not deeply stirred in this earthly life,
Goodness will be implanted
And will work on further within them.

**CAPESIUS**:
    I'd like to speak frankly with you. – – –

## Scene Five

    For many years I've had to admire you,
    But up to now, the strange sense of your
    Peculiar words has remained closed to me, too.

**FELIX BALD:**
    It will certainly disclose itself to you.
    You strive with a noble heart and a good spirit;
    For the times must also come
    When you hear the voice of truth.
    You don't pay heed to how rich in content
    The human being is as an image of cosmic realms.
    Our head is the mirror-image of the heavens;
    Through our limbs work the Spirits of the Spheres;
    In our breast are moving earthly beings;
    And standing over against all these,
    With whose goals they have to clash, are
    Mighty, struggling Demons from the moon's domain. °
    What stands before us as a human being,
    What we experience as the soul,
    What illuminates us as the spirit,
    This hovered from eternity before many of the gods,
    And their purpose was to bind together
    Forces from all the worlds
    Which in unison would form the human being.

**CAPESIUS:**
    I'm made almost apprehensive by these words
    That would boldly view the human individuality
    As an achievement of all the gods.

**FELIX BALD:**
    That's why the greatest humility is necessary
    For those who wish to attain spiritual science;
    And for whoever wants to recognize their self

Simply out of arrogance and vanity,
The gates to wisdom do not open.
*(Felix goes into the house.)*

**CAPESIUS:**

As so often before, surely the good woman Felicia
Will help me this time, too,
So that my soul may direct itself
Towards a picture and warming itself on that
Be able to grasp your words in the right way.

**MRS. BALD:**

Dear Felix has often
Repeated to me, as well,
The words he spoke just now;
They released from my heart
A picture I always told myself
I'd have to tell you.

**CAPESIUS:**

Oh do it, dear woman, – –
I am thirsting for refreshment
From your treasury of pictures.

**MRS. BALD:** °

Well now – – – – –
Once upon a time there was a boy
Who grew up in the lonely solitude of the forest
As an only child of poor woodfolk. –
Apart from his parents,
He got to know but few people.
He was of delicate build;
His skin was almost translucent.
Long could one look into his eyes;

## Scene Five

They held the most profound spirit wonder;
And even though only few people
Ever entered the circle of his life,
The boy did not lack for friends.
When the golden brightness of the sun
Glowed burning on nearby mountains,
Those pondering eyes drew
Spirit gold into the boy's soul,
And his heart became like the morning sun; —
Yet when the rays of the morning sun
Could not break through dark clouds
And a sombre mood was cast o'er all the mountains,
The boy's eyes became dull
And his heart wistful. – –
Thus he was completely given over
To the spirit-weaving of his immediate world,
Which didn't feel more foreign to him
Than the limbs of his own body.
The forest trees and the flowers
Were his friends as well,
For spirit beings spoke
From corona, calyx and crown,
And he could understand their whisperings. – –
Magic things from secret worlds
Disclosed themselves to the boy
When his soul conversed
With what is taken as simply
Lifeless by most people;
And of an evening, his caring parents
Often missed their beloved offspring. –
Then he would be at a nearby place
Where a spring gushed out of the rocky cliffs,
And water drops, dispersing many thousandfold,
Sprayed out over the stones.

## The Soul's Testing

When in a play of colored sparks,
The silver glance of moonlight
Was magically reflected
In the stream of water-drops,
The boy would tarry hours long
Beside the rocky spring,
And shapes, formed spirit-like within
The water's swirling and the moonlight's shimmering,
Arose before the child's seeing eye.
They would grow into the images of three women
Who spoke to him of those things
His soul impulses were inclined towards; –
And when upon one mild summer night
The boy was once more sitting by the spring,
One of the women caught up many thousand droplets
Of that colorful water-drop world
And handed them on to the second woman.
Out of the water droplets
She shaped a silver-glancing chalice
And handed it on to the third woman.
She filled it with the moon's silver light
And then gave it thus to the boy.
All this he beheld
With his child's seeing eye. –
In the night following this experience,
He dreamt how he was robbed of the chalice
By a raging dragon. –
After that night, only three more times
Did the boy experience the magic of the spring;
Thereafter, the women stayed away,
Even when the boy sat pondering
By the rocky spring in the moon's silver light.
And when three hundred sixty weeks
Had flown by for the third time,

## Scene Five

The boy had long grown to be a man
And from his parents' home and woodlands
Had moved into a foreign city.
There, one evening, tired out from hard work,
He sat pondering over what life
Still might have in store for him.
Suddenly the boy felt himself carried away
Back to his rocky spring,
And again he could behold the water-women
And this time hear them speaking.
The first one said unto him,
    "Think on me at those times
    When you feel yourself alone in life.
    I draw the human's eye of soul away
    To etheric distances and the starry widths,
    And whoever would experience me,
    To them I hand on from my magic beaker
    The drink of hope in life." –
And the second one also spoke,
    "Forget me not at those moments
    Threatening your life's courage.
    I direct the human's heart impulses
    To soul foundations and the spirit heights,
    And whoever seeks their forces from me,
    For them I forge with my magic hammer
    The strength of faith in life." –
The third one was thuswise to be heard,
    "Raise your spirit eye up to me
    When life's riddles storm in upon you.
    I spin the threads of thought
    Within life's labyrinths and the soul's depths,
    And whoever puts their trust in me,
    For them I weave on my magic loom
    The rays of love for life." – – –

## The Soul's Testing

In the night following
This experience,
The man dreamed that a raging dragon
Prowled in circles round about him –
And could not come near;
Those beings, that had moved with him
From his homeland to that foreign place,
And on whom he had once looked at the rocky spring,
They guarded him from that dragon.

- - - - - - - - - -

**CAPESIUS:**

Take my thanks, dear woman,
I leave you richly laden with gifts.

*(Stands up and goes. Mrs. Bald goes into the house.)*

*(Capesius alone some distance away, speaking the following.)*

**CAPESIUS:**

I feel how such a picture
Works healingly within my soul
And can restore lost forces to all my thinking.
It was so simple what the woman told,
And yet it arouses thought forces
That carry me off into unknown worlds. – –
In this beautiful solitude,
I shall give myself up to that dreaming
That has so often given my soul thoughts
Which have indeed proved to be far better
Than many a fruit of brooding for weeks on end.

- - - - - - - - - -

*(He disappears behind a dense thicket.)*

## Scene Five

**JOHANNES** (*appears in the same part of the forest, lost in deep contemplation*):
Was it a dream, was it reality? – – –
I cannot bear what my friend said
In her mild quietness, yet so earnestly,
About our separation.
Oh, could I but think that my reason,
Contradicting my spirit's impulse,
Might want to place itself
Between me and her as a deception. –
- - - - - - - - - -

I cannot – I don't want to obey it,
That warning, that Maria found,
To drown out the voice of my soul,
That ceaselessly speaks, "I love her", –
And my love is the well-spring of that work
That alone I want to know about.
What is all that creative drive to me,
What the outlook on lofty spirit goals,
If they rob me of the light
That can illuminate my existence? –
I must be allowed to live in that light;
And if it's taken from me,
Then I simply want death for ever.
I feel how my strength dissolves
When I even try to think:
I would have to wander on pathways
Not illuminated by her light.
- - - - - - - - - -

Before my eyes a haze is being woven
That is beginning to transform the magic
This forest and these cliffs
Otherwise paint so magnificently for my eyes
Into confusion – – –

## The Soul's Testing

A raging dream is emerging from the abyss – – –
*Oh, how it so dreadfully unsettles me – –*
- - - - - - - - - -
Oh, get away from me – – !
I thirst for the solitude
That leaves me my own dreams;
In them I may still strive
For what seems lost to me – –
- - - - - - - - - -
– – It will not move away! – –
Then I will flee from it –
*(Feels himself as if firmly held to the ground.)*
Oh, what chains are holding me
Shackled to this place!
*(The Double of Johannes Thomasius appears.)*
Augh, – – – – – –
Whoever you may be,
Whether human blood is hidden in your form,
Whether your existence is only spiritual –
Leave me – – –
- - - - - - - - - -
Who is it? – – –
A daemon is placing me before myself – – – °
It will not move away; – – – – –
It is the image of my own being, –
It seems to be even stronger
Than this being itself – – – – –

**THE DOUBLE:**
    I love you, Maria ...
    Only with throbbing heart,
    Only with feverish blood
    Can I stand before you. –
    And when your eyes meet mine,

*Scene Five*

    Hot shivers course through me;
    And when you wish to lay
    Your dear hand in my hand,
    Bliss pervades
    All my limbs – – – – – –

JOHANNES:
    You ghostly figure, woven out of misty haze,
    You dare to blaspheme here
    The purest feelings of my heart; – – –
    Oh, what debt have I laden myself with
    That I must look upon
    A lewd caricature of my love,
    That is so sacred to me – – – –

THE DOUBLE:
    I have often listened in on your words, –
    I seemed to have absorbed them into my soul
    As tidings from the Land of the Spirits. –
    Yet more than all those revelations,
    I lovingly sensed your nearness;
    And when you spoke of soul paths,
    Then that bliss pervaded me
    That surges storming in my blood – – –

THE VOICE OF CONSCIENCE:
        So speaks discreetly,
        Yet not repellingly,
        Of appearances avoidingly,
        In the blood permanently,
        The mysterious force
        Of passion.

THE DOUBLE *(in a somewhat other voice)*:
    I am not permitted to leave you;

## The Soul's Testing

You will often find me by your side;
I will not move away from you
Until you have found the force
To make me into the same thing
As the being you are to become.
At this time you are not yet that.
Only in this delusion of your own nature
Can you see it within yourself.

- - - - - - - - - - -

*(Lucifer and Ahriman appear.)*

**LUCIFER:**

O Human, conquer yourself,
O Human, redeem me.
You have overcome me
In your soul's heights;
I remain bound to you
In your being's depths.
You will always find me
On your life's pathways
Should you venture to completely
Shield yourself from me.
O Human, conquer yourself,
O Human, redeem me.

**AHRIMAN:**

O Human, embolden yourself,
O Human, experience me.
You could achieve
The seeing of spirits;
I've had to spoil
The life of your heart;
Still oft you shall suffer
Most intense soul agony

*Scene Five*

    Should you not be content
    To hold to my forces.
    O Human, embolden yourself,
    O Human, experience me.
*(Lucifer and Ahriman disappear, the same for The Double. – Johannes goes into the dimness of the forest in deep contemplation.)*
*(Capesius reappears. From behind the thicket he has participated, as in a vision, in the scene between Johannes and The Double.)*

**CAPESIUS:**
    What happened to me just now? It weighs on me
    Like a dreadful nightmare. Thomasius came this way;
    He seemed to be absorbed in deep contemplation.
    Then he stood still, as if speaking with someone,
    And yet no one other than him was at this place.
    I felt as if a dreadful fear was pressing in on me;
    I didn't see anymore what was happening around me;
    Yet I must have unconsciously, as if sleeping,
    Been completely absorbed in that world of pictures
    I can still quite clearly recollect.
    It must have been only a short time
    I sat thus dreaming, lost in myself,
    And yet how rich was that dream world,
    And how disconcerting it seemed to be.
    I could see people from bygone days
    Quite clearly and also hear them speaking.
    I dreamed about a spirit Brotherhood that strove
    Singlemindedly towards humanity's highest goals.
    I recognized my self quite clearly in their midst
    And felt myself familiar with it all.
    Only a dream, – yet the dream was shattering.
    I certainly know I never could have experienced

## The Soul's Testing

Anything like that within this life;
And what has remained over as impression
Fills my soul just as everyday life does.
It draws me with elemental power to those pictures; –
Oh, could I but behold that dream once again.

(Curtain, while Capesius remains standing.)

The following presents pictures of events from the first third of the Fourteenth Century. Further developments will show that in these events is to be seen the retrospect of their former earthly lives by Capesius, Thomasius and Maria.

## SCENE SIX

A forest meadow. In the background, high rocky cliffs on which a castle stands. A summer evening. Peasants, Simon the Jew, Thomas a Master Miner, a monk.

*(Peasants, six men(M) and six women(W), going over the meadow and, when they pause, speaking.)*

1. PEASANT(M):
    See there, the evil Jew;
    He won't dare to come
    The same way as us;
    He might hear things
    T'would long make his ears itch.

2. PEASANT(M):
    We've got to make it real clear
    Once and for all
    That we'll no longer tolerate
    His audacity in our decent homeland,
    Where he's sneaked in.

1. PEASANT(W):
    He's protected by the high Lords
    Who live up in the Castle;
    None of us are permitted in there,
    The Jew they receive gladly.
    He also does whatever the Knights want.

## *The Soul's Testing*

3. PEASANT(M):

> It's mighty hard to know
> Who serves God and who Hell.
> We should be grateful to our Knights;
> They give us bread and also work.
> What would we be without them?

2. PEASANT(W):

> I really have to praise the Jew.
> By means of his medicines
> He cured me of my grievous illness
> And was so kind and good besides.
> He's often done the same for many others.

3. PEASANT(W):

> But a monk divulged to me
> Its devilish, what the Jew heals with.
> One has to guard against his poison;
> It's supposed to change itself within the body
> And then lets in all kinds of sins.

4. PEASANT(M):

> The people who serve the Knights
> Oppose our ancient customs.
> They say the Jew knows a lot about
> What brings healing and well-being,
> And only in the future will it be valued.

5. PEASANT(M):

> New, better times are coming.
> I already see ahead to them in spirit,
> Where pictures in my soul show me
> What physical eyes can't perceive.
> The Knights want to bring it all about for us.

*Scene Six*

4. PEASANT(W):

> We owe loyalty to the Church,
> Which saves our souls from devilish images,
> From death and the terrors of Hell.
> The Monks warn us to beware the Knights
> And that magician, too, the Jew.

5. PEASANT(W):

> Only a little while longer
> Do we have to patiently bear the yoke
> Laid on us by the Knights.
> The Castle will soon lie in ruins.
> A vision in a dream revealed that to me.

6. PEASANT(W):

> Fear of a grievous sin torments me
> When I so often have to hear
> The Knights want to ruin us. –
> I always see only good coming from them;
> I have to accept them as Christians, too.

6. PEASANT(M):

> How people'll think in the future,
> We should leave to those
> Who come after us.
> As for the Knights, we're simply
> Their instrument for the devilish arts
> By which they oppose
> What is truly Christian.
> When they're driven out,
> We'll be freed from their leadership,
> And then we'll be able to live
> In our homeland according to our own ways.
> Now let's be going to evening service;

## The Soul's Testing

There we'll find what our souls need and
What's in keeping with the customs of our fathers.
The new teachings aren't suitable for us.

*(Peasants exit. Simon the Jew comes out of the forest.)*

SIMON:
So it's simply the same old hate and scorn
I always have to hear on every side,
And yet ever and again I'm filled with pain
When I'm forced to see myself exposed to them.
There doesn't seem to be any reason
For the way I'm being treated by these people,
And yet One thought often recurs
That brings before my soul this truth:
There is meaning in everything we experience.
So there also certainly must be reasons
Why people of my race have to suffer;
And when I look up to the Lords in the Castle,
I find their fate is similar to mine;
Only, they themselves have purposely chosen
What the Rulers of Nature impose on me.
They set themselves apart from all other people
In order, by striving alone, to build up the forces
By which they'll be able to reach their goals.
This is how I feel about what I owe to this destiny
That has blessed me with solitude;
For, being directed only to my own soul,
I have given myself up to the realm of science.
I've been able to recognize from its teachings
How our age is tending towards new goals.
The laws of nature must be revealed to people
Who formerly did not know them;
In this way, they'll conquer the sense world
And let forces unfold from it

*Scene Six*

They'll then have at their service.
I've done what I'm capable of in my own way
To develop the art of healing. This striving
Has made me valuable to the Brotherhood.
The Brothers allow me to search on their lands
For those forces residing in the plants
And to be discovered in the earth's soil and
Which are suitable for new methods of healing.
Thus I labor in accord with their aims and goals
And may well confess that along my pathway
I've been able to joyfully pluck many a fruit.
*(Goes further into the forest.)*


*(Thomas, a Master Miner, comes out of the forest. The Monk comes towards him.)*

**THOMAS:**
I'll set me down here a bit.
My soul needs calm in order to find itself
After storms the like I've been hit by.
*(The Monk comes over.)*

**MONK:**
I greet you right warmly, worthy son.
You've sought out solitude here;
After much work, you want quiet peace
To turn your mind towards spirit worlds.
I'm glad to see my well-loved pupil thus;
But your eye has a wistful look?
It seems that cares torment your soul.

**THOMAS:**
Pain is often near to greatest happiness;
My life has shown this to me in these last days.

## The Soul's Testing

**MONK:**
> Have you then experienced
> Happiness and pain
> All at the same moment?

**THOMAS:**
> My reverend Lord, I have confided to you
> I love the mine Overseer's daughter
> And that she is also deeply fond of me.
> She will take part in life with me as wife.

**MONK:**
> She'll remain true to you in happiness and sorrow;
> She is a piously devoted daughter of the Church.

**THOMAS:**
> Only such a wife could stand by my side
> Ever since I have learnt from you,
> My well-loved guide, true devotion to God.

**MONK:**
> And are you equally sure about your own soul,
> That it will also walk further on the path
> I've been permitted to show you as the right one?

**THOMAS:**
> As truly as my heart beats within my body,
> So truly will your son be faithfully devoted
> For all times to those lofty teachings
> He's been permitted to hear from your mouth.

**MONK:**
> And now you've spoken of your happiness,
> So let me learn also of your sorrow.

## Scene Six

**THOMAS:**
    I've often told you how I've fared. –
    When I had hardly grown out of childhood,
    I began to travel about in the world.
    I often changed my place of work.
    The wish was always alive in my heart
    To meet the father whom I had loved,
    Even though I hadn't experienced good of him.
    He had abandoned my good mother
    Because he wished to win a new life for himself
    Unhindered by wife and children.
    The impulse for adventure was alive in him.
    I was still a child when he left us,
    And my sister was just newborn.
    A short while after, my mother died of grief.
    My sister was put in the care of good people
    Who later left my part of the country.
    I could hear nothing more of the girl.
    Assisted by relatives, I learnt the miner's trade
    And advanced so far in it
    I always found work wherever I sought it.
    Never could the hope leave me
    I would find my father again.
    And now, just when my hope's been fulfilled,
    At the same moment it's been forever taken from me.–
    Yesterday, due to matters connected with my duties,
    I had to report to my superior.
    You know how little I like the Knight
    Who's the supervisor of my work ever since
    It became known to me you are his opponent.
    Ever since then, I've been resolved
    Not to remain in service to the Castle.
    For reasons which remain unknown to me,
    The Knight brought our discussion round

## The Soul's Testing

To such a point that made it possible for him
To reveal himself to me as – my father ...
What followed ... Oh, I'd rather not say ...
I could have forgotten all the sorrow
He caused my mother and myself
As I stood facing my father,
Who spoke of times past, bowed down with pain,
But in him, *your* opponent stood before me.
One thing alone could I be clear about,
What a deep cleft must forever divide me
From him whom I so much wanted to love,
Whom I had so long sought with such yearning. –
I've lost him now for the second time. This
Is how I feel about what I've had to experience.

**MONK:**
I would never want to estrange you
From the bonds laid on you by blood.
Indeed, what I can give to your soul
Shall always be bestowed in love.

(Curtain, while both are exiting.)

## SCENE SEVEN

A room in the castle seen from the outside in the previous scene. Everything is embellished with the symbols of a mystic Brotherhood. The spirit Knights during a meeting; then the Monk with one of the Knights; later the apparition of the spirit of Benedictus, who had died about fifty years before. Lucifer and Ahriman. To begin with, the Grand Master with four Brothers at a long meeting table.

**GRAND MASTER:**
>You, who have become my companions in the quest
>To establish the future goals of humanity
>Which have been given us from the spirit domain
>To carry into the realm of earthly activity
>As the precepts of our Brotherhood,
>You must stand faithfully by my side
>Also in these times of grave troubles.
>Ever since our beloved leader fell
>As sacrifice to those dark Powers
>Which draw their forces from the Evil One, °
>In order in their own way,
>By the force of opposition, to serve wisdom's plan –
>Which works good from evil too – ever since then,
>All our earthly striving has been without hope.
>Our enemies have already overpowered
>A number of our Brotherhood's castles, – –
>And in the fighting many of our beloved Brothers
>Have followed our great Master
>Into the luminous realm of eternity.
>For us, too, the hour soon must strike
>When these walls protectingly enclosing us
>Will also fall.
>Already our enemies are eyeing us on every side

*The Soul's Testing*

As to how they can rob us of the lands and goods
We have acquired, not for our own advantage,
But rather only to make use of
As a means of rallying about us
People into whose souls we can plant
Seeds for the future.
They shall ripen then, when these people
Find their way back from the Land of Spirits
Into a later earthly life.

**FIRST MASTER OF CEREMONIES:**
That our Brotherhood must bow itself
Before the unclear aims of destiny's plans,
This would seem understandable;
But that in its fall our community drags down
The individual lives of so many Brothers,
This seems to be an injustice before cosmic law.
My mouth shall not complain,
For our Brothers died willingly, –
But my soul seeks understanding of the sacrifice
Being demanded of those individuals
Who have bound themselves to a whole
When the Powers of Destiny bring about
The downfall of that whole.

**GRAND MASTER:**
The particular life of each person
Is most wisely linked with the cosmic plan.
Within the ranks of our Brothers,
There is indeed many a one who shows himself capable
Of serving our Brotherhood with his spirit forces,
And yet, he may have flaws in his present existence.°
The erring paths of his heart must find
Their atonement through the sufferings

*Scene Seven*

    He has to bear in service to the whole;
    And whoever, blameless in his own deeds,
    Has to travel the thorny paths
    Arising from the Karma of our Brotherhood,
    On him will the pain bestow the strength
    To rise up to a higher form of life.

**FIRST MASTER OF CEREMONIES:**
    Then does our Brotherhood also tolerate
    Individuals within its midst
    Who can consecrate themselves to its lofty goals,
    Yet without the purist of souls?

**GRAND MASTER:**
    Whoever devotes himself to the higher work
    Weighs only the good in souls
    And leaves the bad to find its own atonement
    In the course of cosmic justice.
    I have called you to me now, my Brothers,
    In order in our days of sorrow
    To remind you with earnest words
    That it behooves us to die joyfully –
    For the goals we have truly sworn
    To dedicate ourselves to in this life.
    You are in the right sense my Brothers,
    When within your souls
    Courageously rings out
    The Brotherhood's Statement of Dedication,
    "Whoever wants to behold spirit goals
    Through senses' revelations,
    Whoever emboldens himself
    To pour spirit will into his own will,
    He must offer up
    His individual existence and his life."

*The Soul's Testing*

**FIRST PRECEPTOR:**
    Exalted Master, would you but test
    The hearts of all our Brothers,
    Then would ring back to you the clearest echo
    Of the words of our Statement of Dedication;
    But we want to hear from your own mouth
    How we are to understand
    That along with our lands and goods, with our lives,
    Our enemies will also rob us of the souls
    We have so lovingly tended.
    Already each day demonstrates more clearly
    How not only through compulsion
    Do our people give themselves over to the victors,
    How they are also learning to hate
    The spirit pathway we have pointed to.

**GRAND MASTER:**
    What we have planted in these souls
    May die for this age,
    But such individuals as have breathed in
    The light of our spirit will return again
    And will then bestow our work upon the world.
    Thus does our great leader often speak
    To my spirit from the Realm of the Dead
    When in my hour of stillness
    I descend into my soul's foundations
    And forces awake in me
    For lingering in the Land of Spirits.
    Then I feel the Master's presence
    And hear his words
    Just as I was so often allowed
    To hear them in our life of the senses.
    He does not speak of the end of our work,
    Only of the fulfillment of our goals

## Scene Seven

In later days on earth.
*(The Grand Master and two brothers exit while two remain behind.)*

**FIRST PRECEPTOR:**
>He speaks of spirit worlds in the same way
>Other people speak about villages or towns. – –
>This way of speaking about other realms
>Of existence by our highest consecrated Brothers
>I find oppressive,
>And yet, I am quite fervently bound
>To all our earthly goals.

**SECOND MASTER OF CEREMONIES:**
>I hold to our Master's words,
>"Whoever cannot hear
>The tidings of the spirit
>And of spirit worlds with full belief –
>He does not lack the ability
>To grasp such revelations.
>He lacks quite other things.
>That he may not feel himself worthy to be
>A member of the higher worlds, he well intuits,
>But would like to keep it hidden from himself.
>The soul must have secret flaws and want
>To deceive itself about them, when it doesn't
>Wish to bow itself before a spirit knowing."
>*(Both exit.)*
>*(The Monk appears in the same room; the Second Preceptor enters to him.*

**SECOND PRECEPTOR:**
>Whatever brings you here into this hall,
>Which you hold as a site of the enemy?

## The Soul's Testing

**MONK:**
> I have to count as one of my friends
> Whatever wears a human countenance,
> So wills our strictest rule;
> But hostile might well appear to you
> What in the line of duty I'm obliged to demand.
> I am here by order of my superiors.
> By peaceful means, they wish to have returned
> The Church's lands, which according to the contents
> Of ancient letters belong to her.
> The piece of land you have reorganized into a mine
> Is rightfully our Church's own property.
> The manner in which you have acquired the land
> Cannot be held as legally right.

**SECOND PRECEPTOR:**
> Whether we can rightfully call it ours or not,
> Over that judges long may argue;
> But it certainly is our own property
> In the sense of a higher right.
> That piece of land was unused ground
> When our Brotherhood bought it.
> It was totally unknown to you
> The depths of that ground hid rich treasures.
> We have won them over for human industry.
> Today this treasure travels
> To farthest lands to further human well-being,
> And many worthy people are working
> In the galleries in that ground – °
> Which you had possessed as wasteland.

**MONK:**
> So, do you not hold it for right
> To actively see that within your Brotherhood

*Scene Seven*

    You peacefully come to an understanding with us
    About how we are to have our rights?

SECOND PRECEPTOR:
    As we are unaware of any guilt,
    Moreover are fully certain of our rights,
    So can we calmly wait
    For whether you will still deign,
    In this matter, too, to add injustice to your cause.

MONK:
    You may attribute it to your own intransigent will
    If we are now forced to other means.

SECOND PRECEPTOR:
    The honor of our Brotherhood demands
    That only in fighting will it
    Let itself be robbed of its rights.

MONK:
    So, then my orders are now fulfilled;
    I can spare both you and myself further words.
    Would it be possible to speak
    To the senior person commanding here?

SECOND PRECEPTOR:
    The Master will certainly be at your service,
    But I ask you to wait a short while,
    He will not be able to come at once.
    *(He exits.)*

MONK:
    Oh, that my office forces me to enter
    The rooms of this hated Brotherhood.

*The Soul's Testing*

On every side my eye encounters
Devilish symbols and sinful images.
A horror seems to want to take hold of me .
It's crackling – oh, it's banging about the room; °
I feel as if surrounded by Evil Powers.
- - - - - - - - - -
Since I am not aware of any sin in me,
I will bid defiance to the adversaries –
- - - - - - - - - -
It's becoming quite terrifying ......
Oh – – – – – –
*(The spirit of Benedictus appears.)*
You good spirits, stand by me!

**BENEDICTUS:**

Consider well, my son!
I was often permitted to turn to you
When the fervor of your prayers
Transported you into the spirit world;
So listen bravely at this moment, too,
To what you must recognize
If spirit brightness instead of darkness
Is to rule within your soul.

**MONK:**

When I pleaded for clarity
In such significant matters as this,
And my devoted prayers
Found a hearing in the Spiritland,
Then you appeared to me, my great Master,
You who were the pride of our order
When he lived in an earthly body.
You spoke to me from higher realms,
Illuminating my mind

*Scene Seven*

And fortifying my strength.
My eye of soul could behold you,
My spirit ear could hear you.
At this moment too, I wish to listen
With devotion to the revelation
You let flow into my soul.

**BENEDICTUS:**
You are in the house of a Brotherhood
Your soul holds guilty of evil heresy.
It seems to hate what we love
And to revere what we deem sin.
Our Brothers take it as their duty
To bring about the downfall of this spirit sin.
For this, they can base themselves on words
I uttered in my earthly existence.
They lack the insight that these words
Can only be livingly productive
If they're continually shaped in the right sense
By those who are the followers of my work.
So let arise within your soul
In the sense of a new age,
What I was permitted to think on earth.
This order, which lets its goals be indicated
To it from out of the realm of mysticism,
Look on it in the light
I myself would see it in
Were it allotted to me
To actively walk among you in an earthly body.
This Brotherhood is directed to higher goals.
The individuals devoted to it
Intuitively sense later earthly ages,
And in premonitions its leaders already behold
The fruits that are to ripen in the future.

## The Soul's Testing

    Science and the guidance of social life
    Will change their forms and goals, and what
    This Brotherhood, which you help to persecute,
    Feels itself driven to achieve in this age
    Are deeds that serve this transformation.
    Only when the goal our Brothers serve
    Is willing to be united for peaceful work
    With the one the heretics are following,
    Can salvation for earthly development blossom.

MONK:
    This warning I've been found worthy of,
    How can I simply follow it? – – –
    It departs mightily from everything
    Appearing to me as correct up till now.
    *(Ahriman and Lucifer appear.)*
    But still other beings are approaching me!
    What do they want at your side?

AHRIMAN:
    The broader wisdom comes from other places.
    It can't seem easy for you
    To obey your predecessor's indications.
    Consider, he lives in the realm of the blessed.
    What there longs for law and duty
    Can only bring about confusion
    Here on earth at the present time.
    Lift up your eyes to his heights
    If you want to seek upliftment
    In a happiness to be granted
    By cosmic spirits in far-off earthly days,
    But if you want to work correctly already now,
    Let only what teaches reason and sense lead you on.
    You have succeeded very well

## Scene Seven

In fathoming the sins of this Brotherhood,
Which they have to hide from the whole world.
They show you how their future precepts
Can quite well live in sinful souls.
With such a science, how could you want
To live in peace with this Brotherhood!
Error is a barren soil
That lets not good fruit ripen.

**LUCIFER:**
Your sense of piety
Has pointed you to the right path.
The goals of the age are certainly changing;
But heretics must not be allowed to predetermine
The paths of the people.
With this spirit Brotherhood,
The danger is it speaks with words of truth
And yet gives the truth that twist
By which it must exceed error
In its dangerousness.
Someone who wanted to openly serve only lies
Would surely have to be seen as fooled by
His own wits were he to live in the belief
People would follow his leadership.
The spirit Knights are not so dumb; –
They do, indeed, speak of the Christ individual,
Because this name opens all the doors
Leading to the souls of the people.
One can best trap the hearts of the people
For the counterimage of Christ
When one gives the name Christ to that image.

**MONK:**
From soul worlds confusingly resound around me

## The Soul's Testing

Voices I have often heard
And yet that always want to fight against
What a sense of piety dictates.
How am I now to find the right paths
If evil powers are praising them to me.
Yet it almost seems like – –
But no, those words, may they remain unthought. –
My wise leader will guide me
So the meaning of his words,
Which seems so dim, can be disclosed.

BENEDICTUS:
I can point out the right path to you
If in your soul depths you permeate yourself
With the words I once spoke on earth;
And if you then will to aspire
To the livingness of those words
In these worlds where you can now behold me,
Then will the right path be pointed out to you.

(The curtain falls while the Monk, the spirit of Benedictus, Lucifer and Ahriman are still in the hall.)

## SCENE EIGHT

The same hall as in the previous scene. The First Preceptor, Joseph Keen, then the Grand Master with Simon, later the First and Second Masters of Ceremonies. Joseph Keen is present to begin with; the Preceptor enters to him.

**FIRST PRECEPTOR:**
    You wished to speak with me. What have you to say?

**JOSEPH KEEN:**
    What has driven me here
    Has significance for both you and for me.
    You know Thomas, the Master Miner?
    He is in service to you here.

**FIRST PRECEPTOR:**
    Of course I know the worthy man.
    We value his clever achievements,
    And all those placed under his leadership
    Are very fond of him.

**JOSEPH KEEN:**
    And of course Cilli, my daughter, you know her, too?

**FIRST PRECEPTOR** (*affected*):
    I have seen her
    When I encountered you with your household. °

**JOSEPH KEEN:**
    Things so came to pass that already
    Quite soon after Thomas arrived here,
    He was very often to be seen in our house.

He has come still more and more often.
We saw he soon formed
The deepest affection for our Cilli.
That wasn't particularly special for us,
But with Cilli's nature, for a long time
We couldn't imagine a requited love.
She always lived only for prayer
And fled from almost all social contact.
It's become increasingly clear, however,
She is devoted with her whole heart
To this foreign man,
And as things stand now,
We've been forced into the position
Of not opposing the wishes of our child,
Who wants to enter into marriage with Thomas.

FIRST PRECEPTOR (*with gestures of uncertainty*):
Why is this marriage against your will?

JOSEPH KEEN:
My noble lord, you know how truly devoted I am
To the spirit of this Brotherhood.
Only with a heavy heart can I bear the fact
My daughter has directed all her love
Towards the other side,
That holds you and I guilty of heresy.
The Monk who now heads the neighboring cloister
And always fights against our Brotherhood's goals
Has completely won over the soul of our daughter.
So long as she is in my house,
The hope will never leave me
She might find her way back
Out of that spiritual darkness to the light,
But I'll have to give her up for lost

*Scene Eight*

If she becomes the wife of this man,
Who just like herself
Seeks human salvation in the sense of that Monk.
The opinions that Father holds,
He has also completely succeeded
In forcing on Thomas as beliefs.
Always only with a shudder could I hear
The curses that flowed from Thomas's mouth
When the talk came round to the Brotherhood.

**FIRST PRECEPTOR:**
We have many enemies,
And it can only be of little moment
Their numbers are increased by one.
What I might have to do with this marriage
Is not illuminated by your words.

**JOSEPH KEEN:**
My noble lord, you see this packet – –
Its contents hold credible testimonies.
Only I and my wife have read them up till now,
Otherwise, they are unknown
To everyone in these parts. At this point,
They must be entrusted to you as well.
The girl who passes as our daughter
Is not mine and my woman's offspring.
We took the child into our care
When her mother passed away.
I think what more you still must hear
Wouldn't seem to make it necessary
To tell you how this all came about.
Long we didn't know the father of our fosterling,
And still to this day Cilli doesn't know
Her origins. She sees in us her true parents.

## The Soul's Testing

It even could've always remained so,
For we love the child as our own.
Many years after the mother's death,
These writings were brought to us
Making it clear who our foster-child's father is.
*(The Preceptor becomes completely uncertain.)*
I don't know whether he is known to you, °
But I'm certain now –
– – – – that you are he yourself.
I don't really need to say a lot more,
But since this has to do with your own blood,
I ask for your support. Perhaps together
We'll succeed in saving the girl from the darkness.

**FIRST PRECEPTOR:**
My dear Keen, you always prove yourself true.
I'd like to be able to count on you still further.
Will it be so, that inside, and outside these walls
Within this district, nobody will hear of
How I stand with respect to this girl?

**JOSEPH KEEN:**
On that I pledge you my word.
I will do you no hurt.
I only ask for your help.

**FIRST PRECEPTOR:**
Understand that I can no longer
Give an account to you at this time.
I ask you to hear me out tomorrow.

**JOSEPH KEEN:**
I will come. – – – –
*(Keen exits.)*

## Scene Eight

**FIRST PRECEPTOR** (*alone*):
How cruelly is my destiny thus fulfilled!
I left wife and child in misery
Because I felt them as fetters.
The paths that vanity showed me
Led me into this spirit Brotherhood.
With words that were high-sounding
I committed myself to this work of human love.
I could do that, burdened with a guilt
Arising from the opposite of love.
The wise human guidance of this Brotherhood
Has clearly been demonstrated on me.
It has taken me into its midst
And given me its strict rules.
I saw myself forced to a self-recognition
Which certainly would have remained
Far from me on other paths of life.
Then, when as by a stroke of destiny
My son moved near me,
I thought higher Powers had compassionately
Let me recognize the way to make atonement.
I have long been aware Keen's foster-child
Is the daughter I abandoned.

- - - - - - - - - -

Destruction stands before the Brotherhood.
The Brothers will consecrate themselves to Death
Conscious that the goals for which
They offer up their lives will live on.
For a long time now I've felt
I'm not worthy of such a death.
Thus, more and more the resolution has grown in me
To make known my situation to the Master
In order to ask him to grant my discharge.
I would then want to devote myself to my children

*The Soul's Testing*

In order in this earthly life
To bring whatever atonement is still possible.
I see it clearly – longing for his father
Did not lead my son here,
Though his good heart believed this.
He was led by the forces of his blood
Binding him to his sister.
The other bonds of blood are shown to be
Loosened by the father's wrong,
Otherwise, that Monk could not have succeeded
In so completely stealing him away from me.
The theft has so well succeeded,
That with the brother, now the sister, too,
Will be estranged from the father.
Thus nothing else remains
But to ensure the children
Now learn the true state of affairs
And then, with resignation, await
The atonement from those Powers
Keeping our life's book of debts. –
*(Preceptor exits.)*
*(After a pause, the Grand Master and Simon enter the hall.)*

**GRAND MASTER:**
From now on you must stay within the castle, Simon.
Ever since they've spread that fairy tale
About sorcery, every step you'd take
In this district would be dangerous.

**THE JEW:**
It really causes me great pain knowing
That people, through their lack of understanding,
Can show themselves hostile to helpful assistance
That only wants to serve their own well-being.

*Scene Eight*

**GRAND MASTER:**
    Whoever, through the grace of higher spirit Powers,
    Is permitted to cast their gaze into human souls,
    They behold therein the enemies who,
    Right within those souls themselves,
    Are opposing their own nature.
    The battle our opponents are preparing for us
    Is only a picture of that great war
    One power within our heart, out of enmity,
    Ceaselessly has to wage against the other.

**THE JEW:**
    My noble Lord, here you are speaking words
    That strike into the very depths of my soul.
    I truly was not born to be a dreamer,
    But when I wander alone through forest and field,
    There often comes before my soul a picture
    I can as little master with my will
    As those things my eyes are looking on.
    A human being places himself before me
    Who wants to lovingly reach out his hand to me.
    In his features, a pain is expressed
    I have never yet seen on any face.
    The greatness and the beauty of that person
    Take hold of all the forces of my soul.
    I want to kneel down and in humbleness
    Devote myself to that messenger from other worlds.–
    Immediately, in the next moment,
    A raging anger flares up within my heart.
    I cannot check the impulse within me
    Igniting my soul's resistance – –
    And I have to shove the hand away
    That is so lovingly held out.
    As soon as reasonableness has returned,

## The Soul's Testing

The figure of light has already withdrawn.
When I later recapitulate in thinking
What is thus often presented to me in spirit,
A thought then comes before my soul
Which shakes me to the depths of my heart.
I feel myself drawn to your teachings
Which make revelation about the Spirit Being
That descended from the sun's realm
And, appearing through the human sensible form,
Wanted to be understood by human hearts;
I cannot close myself to the beauty
Belonging to your noble teachings –
And yet cannot yield my soul to it.
I do indeed have to acknowledge the archetype
Of the human being in your Spirit Being,
Yet contrarily hold myself away from my own being
When I want to trustingly turn myself towards it.
I thus have to experience within myself the war
Which is the archetypal image of all outer battles.
Often I'm made fearful by this difficult riddle
Having to do with the destiny of my whole life:
"How am I to grasp that I understand you,
But cannot yield myself in faith
To the contents of your noble revelation?"
I truly follow the example that you set
And yet am in opposition to everything
Which is the origin and goal of my example;
And when I'm forced to know myself in this way,
Doubt drowns out all faith in ever
Finding myself in this earthly existence;
And often I am even filled
With the fear and worry
That a confused remainder of these doubts
Could extend through all my future earthly lives.

*Scene Eight*

**GRAND MASTER:**
>My dear Simon, the picture you have seen
>Has stood before my spirit in its full light
>As you vividly portrayed it in these words,
>And as you then talked on,
>The picture expanded before my gaze,
>And I was capable of beholding things
>Binding a cosmic goal and a human destiny.
>*(The Grand Master and Simon exit.)*

*(After a pause, the two Masters of Ceremonies enter the hall.)*

**FIRST MASTER OF CEREMONIES:**
>I have to admit to you frankly, dear Brother,
>Our superior's mildness often
>Doesn't seem understandable when I see
>How great the injustice of our enemies is.
>They don't want to hear about our teachings,
>Which they portray gruesomely before the souls
>Of the people as heresy and the Devil's work.
>- - - - - - - - - -

**SECOND MASTER OF CEREMONIES:**
>The Master's mildness flows out of our teachings.
>We must not proclaim as the highest goal in life
>An understanding for all human souls,
>And yet fail to understand our opponents themselves.
>There are many people in their midst
>Who truly live according to the example of Christ.
>Yet even for them, the deepest meaning of our teachings
>Would have to remain closed to their souls
>If they wanted to hear it with outer ears.
>Consider, dear Brother, how you yourself,
>With inner opposition, if only hesitantly,

## The Soul's Testing

Wanted to close yourself off to spirit hearing.
We know from the Masters' revelations,
How by means of spirit light people in the future
Will behold that lofty Sun Being
Who dwelt only once in an earthly body.
We joyfully believe in that revelation
Because we trustingly follow our leaders.
Yet the man we recognize as our superior
Spoke with great significance but a short while ago,
"Your souls must by and by come to maturity
If you want to behold prophetically already now
What will show itself to people only in the future. –
You should not believe", said the Master further,
"That already after your first soul testing,
This foresight of the future will appear to you.
When you have been granted the certainty that all
Human life returns again and again, first then
Will you be confronted with the second testing,
Which loosens the fetters of self-delusion
And lets it spoil the spirit light for you."
And the Master also gave this earnest warning,
"In the stillest moments of devotion, seek often
For how this delusion, as the soul's monster,
Becomes dangerous on the spirit seeker's pathway.
Whoever falls prey to it would like to behold
Their human existence also there
Where the spirit wants to reveal itself
Solely in the spirit light.
If you would worthily prepare yourself
To receive into your eye of soul
The light of wisdom from the Christ individuality,
Then you must keep a careful watch upon yourself
So your own self-delusion may not take you unawares
When your soul believes it farthest off."

## Scene Eight

When we place these words clearly before our eyes,
The false opinion will soon leave us
That in our times, in an easier way,
We can pass on the high teachings
Our souls bear witness to.
We really must feel it as fortunate
We are able to meet so many souls
Who, just in these days, are already unconsciously
Receiving the seed for their future earthly lives;
And this seed can first show itself in a person
As the opponent of those Powers
To which it will later want to turn itself.
In much of the hatred that persecutes us,
I can only discover the seeds of later love.

**FIRST MASTER OF CEREMONIES:**
It certainly is so, that only in such words
Can the goal of highest truth be revealed.
Yet just in these last days, it does seem difficult
To direct our existence entirely in their sense.

**SECOND MASTER OF CEREMONIES:**
There, too, I follow my Master's words.
"It is not granted to the whole of humanity
To live the earth's future existence in advance;
But those individuals must always find each other
Who can behold the nature of later days and who
Wish to consecrate their feelings to those forces
Wanting to rescue all existence from the present
And preserve it for eternity."

(Curtain falls while the two Masters of Ceremonies are still in the hall.)

## SCENE NINE

A forest meadow as in the sixth scene. Joseph Keen, Mrs. Keen, their daughter Bertha; then the peasants; later the Monk; last of all Cecilia, called Cilli, the Keen's foster daughter, and Thomas.

**BERTHA:**
>Mother dear, I would so like to hear from your
>Own mouth the story Cilli often used to talk about.
>You know how to tell all the fairy tales
>Our dear father brings home from the Knights
>And which many people often gladly
>Listen to with the greatest of pleasure.

**JOSEPH KEEN:**
>Fairy tales are a true treasury of the soul.
>What they give to our spirit
>Remains preserved even beyond our death
>And brings forth fruit in later earthly lives.
>They let us dimly intuit what is true,
>And from these intuitions our souls create
>Knowledge needed by us in life.
>Yes, if only the people could understand
>Everything our Knights are giving them.
>Unfortunately, Cecilia and Thomas have
>Only deaf ears for these things now,
>Because they receive their wisdom elsewhere.

**BERTHA:**
>Today I want to hear the story
>That has to do with good and evil.

**MRS. KEEN:**
>I'll most gladly tell it you; listen now:

## Scene Nine

Once upon a time there lived a man °
Who pondered much on worldly things.
His brain was tormented the most
When he wanted to know the origins of evil.
About that, he could give himself no answer.
"The world is from God", – so said he to himself,
"And God can have only good in him.
How can evil people come from good?"
And time and again he pondered all in vain;
The answer didn't want to let itself be found.
Then one day upon his way,
It happened that this brooder
Spied a tree in conversation with an axe.
The axe was saying to the tree,
"What is not possible for you, I can do.
I can fell you; but you, not me."
Then said the tree to the vain axe,
"One year ago a man took from my body,
By means of another axe,
The wood from which he made your handle."
And when the man had heard this speech,
A thought arose within his soul
He could not put clearly into words
But which gave full answer to the question
Of how evil can derive from good.

**JOSEPH KEEN:**

Think this story over, my daughter,
And you will see
How contemplating nature
Can create knowledge in human heads.
I know how much I can clarify for myself
When I spin out further in thinking
The tales by which our Knights instruct us.

BERTHA:
>I am, in truth, a right simple-minded thing
>And would certainly understand nothing
>Of what clever people with learned words
>Could tell about their sciences.
>I even lack all sense for such things.
>I get quite sleepy when our Thomas
>Wants to tell us all about his affairs.
>Yet when my dear father brings home
>His fairy tales from our castle
>And often for hours at a time
>Puts what he has to tell into his own words,
>I could happily listen without end.
>Cilli very often speaks of a sense of piety
>Which in her opinion is lacking in me,
>But I feel true piety
>When I place these fairy tales before my eyes
>And can feel heartfelt pleasure in them.
>*(Joseph Keen, Mrs. Keen and Bertha exit.)*

*(After a pause, the peasants come onto the meadow.)*

- - - - - - - - - -

1. PEASANT(M):
>My uncle just came back home yesterday.
>He's been making an honest living
>For quite a while as a miner in Bohemia.
>He knows plenty to tell of
>That he's heard on his journey.
>The excitement is happening everywhere.
>They're closing in on the spirit Knights.
>Against our Brotherhood, too,
>Everything is already prepared.
>The castle will soon be besieged.

*Scene Nine*

2. PEASANT(M):
>They only shouldn't let it wait too long.
>There'll definitely be plenty of us
>Who'll glady join 'em as fighters.
>I'll be counted 'mongst the first for sure.

1. PEASANT(F):
>You'll be rushing to your own ruin.
>Who could be so lacking in sense
>And not want to think about
>How strongly fortified the castle is.
>The battle will be frightful.

2. PEASANT(F):
>The peasants shouldn't get mixed up
>In things they don't understand.
>Instead of that, some are now roving round
>From place to place in our district
>And right diligently stirring up rebellion.
>Things have already gone so far
>The sick must wail away without care.
>The good man who was formerly a help
>To so many people
>Can no longer leave the castle.
>They beat him up terribly.

3. PEASANT(F):
>Many people were just made very bitter
>When they heard where the sickness came from
>That has broken out among our cattle. –
>The Jew has bewitched it into them.
>He heals people only in appearance
>So that with the forces of Hell
>He can serve the purposes of Evil Powers.

## *The Soul's Testing*

3. PEASANT(M):

   With all that gossip about heresy
   There was little enough to get hold of.
   People had what they needed
   And so couldn't find anything better to do
   Than while away their spare time
   With wicked talk;
   Then someone who knows human nature
   Sent out this made up nonsense
   The Jew might have bewitched our cows;
   That's when the storm really broke loose.

4. PEASANT(M):

   I think all of you should know
   What war and war misery mean.
   Our fathers told us
   What they were forced to endure
   In those times when our land
   Was everywhere occupied by troops.

5. PEASANT(F):

   Time and again I've said it,
   Lordship must disappear.
   A dream has already shown me
   How we can serve the troops
   Which'll come out for the siege
   And look after 'em real well.

6. PEASANT(M):

   Let's not raise the question
   Of whether dreams are still believable.
   The Knights wanted to make us cleverer
   Than our fathers were.
   Now they're about to learn

*Scene Nine*

How much more clever we've become.
Our fathers let 'em in,
We'll chase 'em back out.
I know the secret ways
By which one can get into the castle.
I used to work up there
Until my anger drove me out.
I'll show those Knights
Science can be useful to us.

4. PEASANT(F):

That one isn't thinking good thoughts,
I'm frightened by his talk.

5. PEASANT(M):

How a traitor will lead their enemies
Into the castle by secret paths
Has already been shown me in a spirit picture.

6. PEASANT(F):

I find such pictures quite pernicious.
Whoever can still think in a Christian way
Knows that honesty
And not treachery
Will free us from the Evil One.

6. PEASANT(M):

I let people talk
And then do what can be of use.
Certainly, many condemn as wrong
What they can't carry out themselves
Because they haven't got the courage;
But let's be going on now.
The Father is already coming along the path.

## The Soul's Testing

We wouldn't want to disturb him. —
Up till now I could so easily
Follow him in everything,
But today, many of the words in his sermon
Just weren't understandable to me.
*(The peasants go off towards the forest.)*


*(After a pause, the Monk comes over the meadow path.)*

**MONK:**
The soul's paths must become confused
If she wants to follow her own nature.
Only the weakness of my heart could have placed
Those delusory figures before my eyes
When I was in that hall;
But that they had to place themselves before me
In conflict, simply shows how little, even now,
My soul forces are able to unite within me.
I must thus strive anew
To enflame within me those words
That send me light from the spirit heights.
Only they can crave for other paths
Whose mind is kept blind by their own delusion.
The soul can only overcome deception
When she proves herself worthy of that grace
Wanting to reveal the spirit light to her
In words of wisdom from the well-spring of love.
I know that I will find you, you noble force
That can illuminate our Fathers' teachings,
When with a piously devoted heart I can
Escape the darknesses of my own self-conceit.
*(The Monk exits.)*
*(After a pause, Cecilia, called Cilli, and Thomas come onto the meadow.)*

## Scene Nine

CECILIA:
>My dear brother, when often in silent prayer
>I ardently bowed down with my whole soul
>To the well-spring of the world, and the
>Longing to be united with it filled my heart,
>There came before my spirit a shining light. –
>Out of it streamed a mild warmth.
>The shining light then formed itself into a picture
>Of a human being who looked on me with gentle eyes,
>And words sounded forth from that picture.
>They rang out thus:
>"You were forsaken once through human delusion,
>You will be born up now through human love,
>So wait until your longing can find
>The way to lead it to you."
>So spoke that human image quite often to me.
>I couldn't find the meaning of its words
>But was heartened by the dim intuition
>That one day it would be fulfilled;
>And then when you, dear brother, came,
>And I could see you for the first time,
>I felt my strength of mind evaporate –
>You resembled that human countenance exactly.

THOMAS:
>The dream and intuition were not deceiving you.
>Your longing was leading me to you.

CECILIA:
>And when you desired me for your partner,
>I believed you were intended for me by that Spirit.

THOMAS:
>That that Spirit wanted to lead us together,

## The Soul's Testing

Is shown us, in truth, with full clarity,
Even though we misunderstood it at first.
As if it wanted to bestow a wife on me,
So did it seem when I got to know you.
I found again the sister lost at an early age.

**CECILIA:**
And now nothing shall separate us any more.

**THOMAS:**
And yet, how much is placed between us!
Your step-parents are so closely bound up
With that Brotherhood I must reject.

**CECILIA:**
They are completely filled with love and goodness;
In them you'll have good friends.

**THOMAS:**
My beliefs will separate me from them.

**CECILIA:**
You will find the way to them through me.

**THOMAS:**
Good Keen has a rigid mind.
Indeed, what the source of all light is for me,
He will always count as simply darkness.
First in my mature years was I allowed
To turn myself towards this light of truth.
What I had heard of it as a child
Had hardly become conscious for my spirit,
And later I was only concerned to properly
Learn the science that was to support my life;

## Scene Nine

And first here could I find the guide
Who was able to set my soul free.
The words he lets me hear
Bear the genuine marks of all truth.
He speaks in such a manner heart and head alike
Must give themselves over to the teachings
He, full of mildness and goodness, gives out.
Previously, I had made the greatest efforts
To clarify that other spirit path for myself.
I found that it would have to lead to error.
It only holds to those spirit forces that
Do indeed guide reliably within earthly impulses,
But that cannot lead to higher worlds;
And now, how am I to find the way
To the hearts of people like these who simply
Want to await all salvation from this error.

**CECILIA:**
I hear your words, dear brother;
They do not seem inspired by peace.
For me, however, they have let an image of peace
From earlier days come before my soul.
It was on Good Friday, many years ago,
When I also saw that picture of which I just spoke.
The man who bore my dear brother's features
Said to me at that time,
"The human soul arose from divine existence. Dying,
She can dive down into the foundations of her being.
One day she will release her spirit from death."
First later did I become clearly aware
This is the maxim of our Knights.

**THOMAS:**
Oh sister, so now this evil saying

My opponents take as the content
Of their highest spirit truth
Must sound forth to me from your mouth.

CECILIA:
At heart, I'm completely averse
To the outer deeds of this company of Knights
And true to the beliefs that edify you;
Yet never could I persuade myself that people,
Who as the goal of their teachings had in this way
Marked out a path for their soul, are not
To be seen as walking in the footsteps of Christ.
I am a truly devoted student of the spirit
And must confess I wish to believe
That on that day my brother's spirit
Wanted to speak of the goals of soul peace.

THOMAS:
The goals of soul peace do not seem destined
For our life by the Powers of Destiny;
They took our father from us
At that very hour they gave him back.

CECILIA:
When I hear you speak of father like this,
Pain robs me of all clarity of mind.
Your heart draws you lovingly to him,
And yet you shudder when you want to think about
Still being united with him in this life.
You follow loyally our wise guide
And cannot hear when the message of love streams
So warm-heartedly through the force of his words.
I feel myself before a dark riddle;
I see your good heart and your beliefs

*Scene Nine*

    And can only stand trembling before the abyss
    That deepens frighteningly between them;
    And if there did not live in me the comforting hope
    That love will always prove itself victorious,
    I would lack the courage to bear this sorrow.

THOMAS:
    It is still hidden from you, dear sister, how
    Compellingly the force of thought displays itself
    When it totally takes hold of a person's soul.
    Not against his father does this son now stand;
    Thought turns itself away from thought. – –
    I feel the power of this force within my soul.
    To set myself against it would be
    The true spirit death of my own being.

(The curtain falls while Thomas and Cecillia are still on the meadow.)

The following is the continuation of the events portrayed in the first five scenes.

## SCENE TEN

The same landscape as in the fifth scene; Capesius is awakening out of the *vision* which has placed his former incarnation before his soul. °

**CAPESIUS:**
>Oh these strange surroundings! A bench,
>A cabin and a forest clearing before me ...
>Do I know them? They insistently demand
>That I do know them. They press in upon me.
>They lay themselves on me like heavy weights.
>They seem to be reality; but no, all this –
>Is nothing but a picture woven out of soul material.
>I know how these pictures were fashioned
>From my longing and from my soul thirst.
>I've emerged, as if awakening, out of that longing –
>And out of that wide-spread spirit ocean.
>With a frightful shudder rises up out of my
>Soul foundations memory of that longing. How its
>Thirst for a world of concrete existence did burn. –
>The delusory desire coming from that privation
>Burned away my whole individuality.
>I had to passionately crave for existence, and
>Every concrete existence could only flee from me.
>One moment, that seemed an eternity to me,
>Poured into my soul storms of agony
>Only a whole lifetime could bring,
>And then what, *before* that terror of longing,
>Had created that terror, stood before me.
>I felt myself expanded to the whole universe

## Scene Ten

And robbed of all my own individuality, – but no,
That was not I who experienced that so, that was
Another being who arose from me. I saw a human being
And the doings of human beings growing out of
Cosmic thoughts that were hurrying through space
And, coming to being, pressed through to manifestion.
Those thoughts placed one life's whole world,
Graspable in pictures, before my eyes.
They took the strength from my soul material
In order to create existence out of thought.
The more that world before me could condense itself,
The more I myself lost of my own feelings,
And words sounded forth from that world of pictures,
Pressing in upon me, thinking themselves.
They created beings from my life's shortcomings
And gave them strength from my good deeds.
They rang out warningly from the widths of space,
"O human, recognize yourself within your world."
I saw a being that, placed before me,
Showed me my soul as that of his,
And then those cosmic words spoke on,
"So long as you cannot think this being as
Completely interwoven in all your life circuits,
You are but a dream, only dreaming your self."
I couldn't think in clear forms, only actively
Behold forces that confusedly pressed themselves
From nothingness into existence,
From existence into nothingness.
Yet when I strive in spirit further backwards,
Remembering what I beheld previous to that,
There stands before my soul the picture of a life
Which is not so confusing as everything was
I then experienced in those later moments, which
Clearly shows me much more distinctly a human being

## The Soul's Testing

And the doings of human beings in all their details.
In that picture is confided to me
Who those people are and what they are doing.
I know all the souls I can look upon,
But their bodily forms are shaped differently.
I look on all that as if I myself had to experience
Myself as a being of that world, and nevertheless,
What stands before me similar to fully real life,
Leaves me cold and without feelings.
It seems as though the effect upon my soul
Held itself over for that latter moment
Which then stood before my spirit earlier.
I could quite easily recognize myself and
Other people in the midst of a spirit Brotherhood,
But now, like a picture from olden times experienced
As something wrested from memory's well-spring.
I look on Thomas, my son, as miner,
And then have to call to mind the human soul
Otherwise shown me as Thomasius.
The woman whom I know as a seeress
Comes before my eyes as child of my own body.
Maria, who befriends Thomasius,
Is revealed in the robe of the Monk
Who condemns our spirit Brotherhood,
And Strader wears the face of Simon the Jew.
In Joseph Keen and in his woman
I see the souls of Felix and Felicia.
I can quite clearly survey the lives
Of the other people and my own as well;
Yet when I now completely give myself over to it,
Everything again disappears for my spirit.
I can sense how the soul material
From which that picture was woven
Is pouring itself back into my own soul,

*Scene Ten*

Yet I feel myself taken hold of
In my whole being by blessedness.
I seem to be set free from the senses' limitations.
My existence has expanded to the whole universe. —
This is how I feel about that long moment
I was able to live through ere I found myself
Placed before that picture of a former life;
And now I can behold still further back; —
Condensing out of the force of that cosmic thought,
There now appears before my eyes the forest,
The house in which Felicia and Felix
Have so often afforded comfort in my life's troubles.
And now — I find myself again within the world
From which I just now experienced myself displaced
By earthly ages and by cosmic distances; and
What I could still behold before, without feeling,
The picture, which had revealed me to myself,
That now is laid like hazy soul forms
In front of everything my senses are experiencing.
This picture is becoming a nightmare that presses
In upon me. It writhes in the depths of my soul.
- - - - - - - - - -
It opens up cosmic portals, space distances -
- - - - - - - - - -
What is storming into my being's foundations?
What is pressing into me from cosmic distances?

A VOICE AS SPIRITUAL CONSCIENCE:

> Feel what you have beheld,
> Experience what you have done,
> You are now newly arisen for this existence. —
> You have been dreaming your life.
> Create it for yourself

Out of noble spirit light;
With your soul's force for seeing,
Recognize what is yours to do
In this existence.
If incapable of this,
You'll be bound for eternity
To an unreal nothingness.

(The curtain falls while Capesius is still present.)

## SCENE ELEVEN

The same meditation room as in the second scene. Maria, Ahriman.

**AHRIMAN:**
With what artfulness has Benedictus spun
The threads of thought you've been following.
They've certainly entangled you in error.
Thomasius, and Capesius as well,
Are victims of the same delusory sight.
As with yours, their gaze has fallen
On lives in long past days of earth.
Since then, you all seek in former times
For the existence preceeding your present one.
If you allow yourselves in this manner
To determine for this earthly path
Duties which will then be the consequences
Of what you've learned in delusion,
You'll simply be breeding error on error.
That Benedictus merely took those pictures
Out of your own brain and set them in earlier times,
This you can clearly discover from what you know.
You saw the people in that ancient time
Hardly different from those of your own day.
You saw men as men and women as women,
And their traits of character were similar as well.
Hence for you there can no longer be doubt
You shifted back into dim antiquity
With your spirit eye, not the truth,
Rather only the delusion of your own soul.

**MARIA:**
I look on you as the Father of All Deception,
Yet I also know you often speak the truth,

## The Soul's Testing

And those who reject all the advice they can obtain
From your words become victims of the worst error.
Just as delusion makes use of the mask of truth
In order to be sure of ensnaring our souls,
So can we easily give ourselves up to deception
If all we want to do is always sneak past
All sources of error in cowardly fear.
Not for delusion alone is the soul thankful to you;
From the Spirit of Deception also descends the power
That bestows the strength for sure judgement on us.
That is why I want to place myself
In independence over against you.
You have taken hold in that part of my soul
Which must always preserve itself by wakefulness.
When I weigh up all the reasons you, with
Clever calculation, reproached me with just now,
Only an image fashioned by my own brain seems
To have been set back into earlier days on earth;
Yet I ask you whether your wisdom is able
To open the gates to all earthly ages?

AHRIMAN:

In no spirit realm do any beings live
Which hostilely set themselves against me
When I need entrance into earthly ages.

MARIA:

The lofty Powers of Destiny have wisely
Appointed you as their Adversary.
You further everything you wish to hinder.
When you penetrate to the soul's foundations,
You bring our human souls the power of freedom.
From you arise the forces of thought, which indeed
Are the origin of deceptive figments of knowledge,

*Scene Eleven*

But are also the guides for our sense of truth.
There is but One region in the Land of Spirits
Where that sword can be forged before whose sight
You must withdraw, and that is the realm
Where our souls fashion for themselves
A knowledge from the forces of understanding
And then transform it into spiritual wisdom;
And if at this moment I can rightly forge
That sword from words of truth,
You will be forced to withdraw from this place.
So hear me now, you who are the Father of Deception,
Whether I speak all-conquering truth before you.
There are certain times in earthly development
When old forces must slowly die away, and while
Dying, new ones can already be seen growing.
As they were seeking their earlier earthly lives,
My friends, and I, found ourselves united in spirit
At just such a turning point in time.
True spirit individuals were working then
Who bound themselves together in soul brotherhood
And took their goals from the realm of mysticism.
In those earlier earthly days,
Seeds that need a long time to fully ripen
Were carefully planted into human souls.
In their next life, such individuals will still show
Some traits of character from the earlier one.
There will be many men from a time like that
Who become men again in their next life,
And many women will again become women.
The length of time that lies between their lives
Is then also shorter than otherwise.
You lack a sure eye for such turning points,
Thus you're not capable of
Surveying their development without error.

*The Soul's Testing*

>Recall how we encountered each other
>In the house of that spirit Brotherhood,
>And you spoke words, flattering to my deepest soul,
>Which were supposed to set my sense of self free.
>Remembrance of that time now bestows on me
>The strength to set myself against you.

*(Ahriman withdraws with a reluctant gesture. Thunder.)*

**MARIA:**
>So, he has had to withdraw from this site
>Which has so often received Benedictus's blessing;
>For me, however, was wonderfully revealed
>How easily error can happen in souls who
>Depart from safe pathways and open themselves
>Without wakefulness to spirit hearing.
>The Adversary has strong forces
>To emphasize the contradictions in our life
>And thus to rob our souls of certainty.
>He must fall silent when the light appears
>Illumining from the well-spring of wisdom itself
>And bestowing brightness on our spirit vision.

*(Curtain falls while Maria is still in the room.)*

## SCENE TWELVE

The same room as in the previous scene. Johannes and Lucifer.

**LUCIFER:**
    In Capesius, recognize the fruits
    That must ripen when the soul wants to open
    Itself to the spirit domain too early.
    He knows now the words written in his book of life
    And what is incumbent on him for many lives to come;
    But sufferings not intended by destiny's plan
    Arise from a knowledge that lacks the forces
    To transform itself into deeds in life.
    Whether this or that can succeed
    Depends upon the ripeness of a person's will.
    With every step he takes in life,
    Capesius will now have to ask himself,
    "Am I also fulfilling all the dictates of duty
    Arising for me out of that earlier life?"
    Thus, over everything a light is spreading
    That will painfully blind his eyes
    And yet can nevermore help him.
    It deadens the forces that are the sure guides
    For the human soul within its unconscious part,
    And yet it cannot enhance thoughtfulness.
    Thus it simply lames the body's strong power
    Before the soul can master it.

**JOHANNES:**
    I can see the error of my life.
    I stole my soul force from my body and
    Bore it proudly into the spirits' lofty realms;
    But not a complete human being
    Was led to the light on that path;

## The Soul's Testing

It was only a faint shadow of the soul that
Could become enraptured with those spirit expanses
And feel itself at one with the Powers of Creation.
It wished to live in blessedness with the light
And behold in colors, the deeds of light.
As artist, I thought to creatively reproduce
Spirit existence within the senses' worlds.
That being that borrowed its features from me
Has shown me to myself with terrifying truth.
I dreamed only of purest soul love,
But in my blood raged passion. —
I have now been permitted to survey the earthly
Path that is the genuine creator of this life.
It shows me how I should truly strive.
And the spirit pathways I've been travelling?
How could the soul ever follow them
That prior to its present earthly path
Found its sheath in Thomas's body?
How he fashioned his life then
Must place my goal before my eyes now.
In this existence I wanted to achieve
What can only really come to fruit later.

**LUCIFER:**
My light must now securely lead you on,
Just as you let yourself be led by it till now.
The spirit pathway you have entered on,
It can wed the spirit to the higher world,
But it brings darkness to your soul.

**JOHANNES:**
What has a man achieved who has to give himself
Over to the Land of Spirits all soulless!
At the end of all his times on earth

*Scene Twelve*

    He would only be that same being he was
    When at the very beginning his human form
    Was permitted to emerge from the cosmic womb.
    If I were to give myself over to those urges
    From the unconscious depths of my soul that are
    Powerfully pressing for concrete expression in life,
    The whole universe would have an effect upon me.
    I don't now know what's driving me on to act,
    But surely it's the cosmic will itself directing me
    Onward towards its goals, and it must know what this
    Life should be, even if my knowledge can't fathom it.
    What it creates within the whole human being
    Are our life's treasures, which fashion the soul.
    I want to give myself over to them
    And not deaden them further by vain spirit striving.

LUCIFER:
    I am active within that cosmic will
    As it powerfully streams through human souls.
    So long as they cannot fully experience me,
    They are but a limb on a higher individuality.
    I only make the soul into a true human being when
    It can, as self, fit itself into the whole universe.

JOHANNES:
    For a long time now, I thought
    I knew you completely, but only a phantom
    Lived within me which the spirit vision
    From you had previously fashioned for me.
    I must experience you, must willingly live you,
    Then I'll also be able to overcome you in the future
    When my plan of destiny wills to so ordain it.
    Let the spiritual learning I achieved early on
    Henceforth rest within my soul foundations

Until my life's urges themselves awaken it.
With fullest trust I give myself over
To that will that is wiser than the human soul.

(Johannes exits with Lucifer.)

## SCENE THIRTEEN

The Sun Temple; the Hierophants' hidden site for the Mysteries. Lucifer, Ahriman, the three soul figures. Strader, Benedictus, Theodosius, Romanus, Maria. Lucifer and Ahriman enter first.

**LUCIFER:**
>As victor stands the Lord of All Desire before you, –
>We have been able to conquer that soul °
>That even in the light of the Spirit Sun
>Has had to feel itself related to our realm.
>At the critical moment, I could still
>Bedazzle its eye for that shining light
>It had given itself up to only while dreaming.
>Yet when I now turn to my comrade in arms,
>All hope that victory in the domain of the spirit
>Can be won by us must vanish once again.
>You could not conquer for yourself the soul
>That was to lead our efforts to our goal. –
>Thus only for short earthly periods
>Will I be able to hold
>Without purpose in our realms
>This human soul that has surrendered itself to me;
>Then it will have to be returned to our opponents.
>For complete victory, the second one,
>Who has eluded your efforts, is necessary. °

**AHRIMAN:**
>The time is not propitious for my efforts,
>I find no means of access to these souls.
>Already One approaches whom I've greatly agitated.
>It is here still without knowing the spirit, even
>Though a powerful impulse to understand leads it on.
>Thus I must give way to it at this place,

## The Soul's Testing

Where it can only enter unconsciously.
*(The three soul figures enter with Strader.)*

**PHILIA:**
> I shall fill myself with
> The luminous power of faith,
> From joyous soul striving
> I shall breath into myself
> The living strength of trust,
> So the light may awaken
> This slumbering spirit.

**ASTRID:**
> I shall weave together
> Received words of revelation
> With humble soul joy.
> I shall intensify
> The raying out of hope.
> In darkness will shine light,
> In light will enter darkness, °
> So these forces may bear
> This slumbering spirit.

**LUNA:**
> I shall warm the soul's light
> And shall firm up love's power.
> They will embolden themselves,
> They will redeem themselves,
> And raising themselves up,
> Want to give themselves weight,
> So its worldly burdens
> Leave this slumbering spirit,
> And his soul's desire for light
> May set him free forever. °

## Scene Thirteen

*(Enter Benedictus, Theodosius and Romanus.)*

**BENEDICTUS:**
>I have summoned you who are my companions
>In the search for that spirit light
>That is to flow to human souls.
>You know the nature of the soul's sun;
>How often it shines at fullest midday brightness,
>At other times, setting, it penetrates only weakly
>Into the haze of soul dreams
>And thus must often give way to the darknesses.
>The spirit sight of a temple servant must penetrate
>To those soul depths into which the spirit light
>From lofty cosmic places strongly shines;
>However, it must also find those dim goals
>Unconsciously wanting to steer a human being's
>Forces for development into soul darknesses.
>The spirit beings which give human souls
>Spiritual sustenance from the cosmic Powers,
>They are now present in this holy Temple
>In order to direct the goal of one man's soul
>From spirit night into the realm of exalted light.
>He is still enveloped in the sleep of knowledge,
>But spirit calls have already rung out
>In the unconscious substrata of his being.
>What they are speaking in the depths of his soul
>Will soon penetrate to his spirit hearing, too.

**THEODOSIUS:**
>Until now, this soul has not been able
>To find itself again within the spirit light
>That shines through the senses' manifestations
>And reveals the meaning of all earthly development.
>It saw the divine spirit divested of nature

## The Soul's Testing

And what is natural estranged from the divine.
Thus through many earthly lives it had to place
Itself in estrangement over against the meaning of
Its existence and could always only find such a
Bodily sheath as instrument for its own being
As separated it from the world and human beings.
In this Temple, this soul will now acquire the force
To perceive this estranged existence as its own
And thus also be able to win the power
To lead it out of thought's labyrinths
And show it pathways to the well-springs of life.

**BENEDICTUS:**

Another man is striving for the Temple's light;
Only in the future will he approach our gates
And want to enter this sacred place.
In an earnest life of research, he has planted
Many seeds of thinking into his soul foundations.
Thus, the spirit light had to reach those seeds
And let them ripen outside the Temple.
He has been able to behold how his present
Earthly existence shows itself as consequence
Of another he experienced in times long past.
He has now become fully conscious
Of the errors in that life and their effects.
He lacks the strength to fulfill the obligations
He now can feel through his self-recognition.

**ROMANUS:**

By means of the power of this Temple,
Capesius is to recognize how in One earthly life
A person burdens himself with obligations
Only then requited in full measure
By means of many earthly pilgrimages.

*Scene Thirteen*

In this way, he will be able to acknowledge
Without fear that his soul must ever bear the
Consequences of old errors through the gate of death.
He will be able to prove himself victor
In the fight to open the spirit's gates
When he boldly looks in the eye of the Guardian who
Stands before the Threshold of the Land of Spirits.
The Guardian will then reveal to him that nobody
Reaches the heights of life if the book of destiny
Telling of their own existence makes them fearful.
With courage he will come to the conclusion
That self-recognition must beget sufferings
For which it itself knows no words of consolation.
Then shall that will become a companion to him that
Bravely gives itself to the future and, strengthened
By the forces at the well-spring of hope, places
Itself over against the sufferings of recognition.

**BENEDICTUS:**
    As our Temple's truly devoted servants,
    You, my brothers, have marked out in your wisdom
    At this hour the pathways on which
    You will be able to guide to their goals
    The souls of both these spirit seekers.
    Our service in this Temple demands still other work.
    You see here at our side the Lord of All Desire
    Who is permitted to enter this hallowed site
    Because Johannes's soul could open for him
    The gates otherwise closed to him.
    This Brother, to whom we gave our consecration,
    Still lacks at this time the strength
    To courageously put up resistance to the words
    Being created from out of his darknesses.
    His good forces will first strengthen for him if

They rightly experience themselves on their opposite.
Thus he will soon be warmly embraced again
By brotherly love within our Temple.
Yet since he wants to descend into his darknesses,
His spirit treasure must be watched over.
*(Turning towards Lucifer.)*
To you must I now turn, who not for long
May rule the place where you are standing.
The power of this Temple still cannot wrest
Johannes's soul from you at this time,
But in future it will be ours again
When those fruits ripen for our Sister
Which we can already recognize by their blossoms.
*(Maria appears.)*
She was permitted to see in her past earthly life
How Johannes was bound to her.
He was following her lead already in those days
When she herself still wanted to resist
The light to which she now is fully devoted.
If these soul bonds prove to be so strong
They outlast the transformation of the spirit,
Then the power of the Lord of All Desire
Will certainly have to shatter on their firmness.

**LUCIFER:**
It was Benedictus's own will that had to separate
The souls of Johannes and Maria,
And where individuals are severed from one another,
There the field is well prepared for my power.
I'm always searching for severed soul existences
In order to liberate such an independent earthly
Existence from all cosmic servitude forever.
In the frock of a monk, the being that was
Maria had turned away from his father

## Scene Thirteen

The soul now living in Johannes's bodily form.
This has also prepared seeds
I can certainly bring to ripeness.

MARIA (*turned towards Lucifer*):
  There are sources of love in the human being
  To which your powers cannot penetrate.
  They are laid open when ancient errors of one life,
  Which we have unconsciously burdened ourselves with,
  Are looked upon by our spirit in a later earthly life
  And are then, by freely-given sacrifices of will,
  Transformed into deeds in that life
  That may bear fruit for true human benefit.
  The Powers of Destiny have willed to give me
  The sight by which ancient days are visible,
  And signs have also already been given me
  Teaching me to direct my sacrifices of will
  So that benefit may arise for those human souls
  With whose life threads mine must always
  Be connected within earthly development.
  In his former earthly body,
  I saw Johannes's soul turn away from his father,
  And I saw the Powers that drove my self
  To estrange the son from the father's heart.
  Thus, the father now stands over against me,
  Warning me of the debts of that ancient life.
  He clearly speaks in those cosmic words
  That are created as signs in our life's deeds.
  What I have placed between the father and the son
  Had to reappear, though now in another form,
  Within *this* life, which has once again
  Bound Johannes's soul closely with mine.
  I can recognize in all the pain I had to bear
  When I had to sever Johannes from me

## The Soul's Testing

The destiny-laden consequences of my own deeds. —
If my soul can remain true to the light
The spirit Powers are bestowing on it,
It will create forces for itself through
The service it is capable of rendering Capesius
On his present life's difficult pilgrimage.
With the forces thus earned, it will then
Certainly also be able to behold Johannes's star
When he, diverted by the chains of desire,
Does not tread the path the light shines on.
My soul will recognize from the spirit vision
That guided it in those distant earthly days
How it is to fashion our soul bonds at *this* time,
So that the forces for life, having been
Prepared in a state of dulled awareness,
May work on in the sense of human benefit.

**BENEDICTUS:**
In ancient days on earth
A knot was formed from the threads
That Karma spins in world development;
Three human lives were there interwoven.
Exalted spirit light from this hallowed site
Is now shining on this knot of destiny.
To you, Maria, I must now turn;
Of all those souls, only you alone
Are now at this Place of Sacrifice.
May this light work on within your self,
Creating healing for the forces
That once, in one of life's knots, tightly bound
The threads of your life to those of the others.
In that earlier existence,
The father could not find the heart of his son,
But now this spirit seeker is to accompany

## Scene Thirteen

Her friend's self on its path into the Spiritland,
And for you arises the duty to maintain Johannes's
Soul within the light through your own strength.
The way you once chained it to you, only allowed it
To follow you in a state of dulled awareness.
You handed it back its freedom
When it was still given over to you in delusion.
You will find your friend's soul once again
Since it itself now wants to win its own character.
If your soul remains true to the light
The Powers of the Spiritland are bestowing on you,
Johannes's soul will thirst for that of yours
Even in the realm of the Lord of All Desires,
And through the love that binds it to you,
It will again find the path to that exalted light.
For a being permitted to knowingly look on
Spirit heights out of its own soul depths
Can livingly penetrate both light and darkness.
It has breathed in the air from cosmic distances
That is enlivened with life for all eternity, – –
And, in that it is living, raises all human existence
Out of soul foundations to the sun's heights. – –

(Curtain falls.)

# TRANSLATOR'S NOTES

The title **The Soul's Testing** is intended to convey that at certain stages of their life, individuals must experience a real, yet inner, soul testing which they must win through if they are to go forward in their inner development. In modern terms, such a testing may be seen as the limit or barrier of the unknown, both in the outer world and what is unknown within our soul, that needs to be overcome or penetrated in order to arrive at new fields of knowledge or a new configuration for our soul. Certainly, we as individuals, and our society as a whole, have well known limits to what we call reality, and when there are social, moral or religious values placed on these limits, they are often made into barriers we are unwilling to cross. But social development moves on, and what at one time is taboo, at another becomes acceptable or even necessary.

Rudolf Steiner's Mystery Dramas can be seen as guides to breaking through certain barriers and limits. Soul and spiritual realities are presented on the stage which cannot be seen or understood by us as such, precisely because we have not successfully passed through the necessary tests. Without having arrived at the new field of knowledge or understanding, what is presented may well appear in part as chaotic, ridiculous or impossible; yet precisely by seeking in this chaotic, ridiculous or impossible, we can develop unknown forces within our souls which then do let us fathom these pictures in a new way. To successfully pass this soul testing requires a new, unknown effort on our part, and this drama purports to show how a few modern individuals carried through such an effort.

Precisely the ideas of the recurrence of earthly life for one individual and the possibility of consequences in one life arising from another life, are not fathomable and therefore believable on the basis of our society's present type of knowledge. With such ideas, an entirely new approach to social values, personal morality and religious sentiments forces itself upon us. An understanding of Karma would indicate we are not only responsible for what we do, but the outer conditions under which we live, indeed, what we inherit from our families, may also be a direct result of what we were and what we did. What will come for us far into the future may depend on how we act now. To win through the soul testing indicated in this drama may also thus be seen to involve a question of courage, an inner soul courage for truths which need to be awoken to life.

The scenes (**6** to **9**) of the Fourteenth Century are not to be understood as simply made up out of fantasy. Just as it was explained in the First Drama how the characters were taken from concrete individuals whom Rudolf Steiner had met or studied, so here the historic portrayal is taken from the real historic situation of that time and place; yet again here, it is presented through archetypal soul and spiritual pictures which are necessarily imbedded in an historical situation.

The historical basis of the Brotherhood was the Knights Templar. Masters of Ceremonies were responsible for the cultic ceremonies and internal moral/social order. Preceptors were those responsible for the worldly goods of the order, often including land areas or provinces. 'our beloved leader' (s.7, p. 215) was Jacques de Molay who was burned at the stake in Paris in 1314. Research indicates the castle portrayed in the scenery was located in eastern Austria-Hungary and was attacked and fell about 1320/35. The Monk is of the Dominican Order, and his beloved leader, who was the 'pride of our Order' (s.7, page 222), was almost certainly Thomas Aquinas 1226-1274 who was known as Doctor Angelicus.

Just as an attempt to grasp the inner realities of individuals through the soul and spiritual pictures in the first drama would help us to develop the ability to fathom ourselves, so here too, the attempt to grasp these soul and spirit pictures out of past situations forces us to seek for the streams of development the dramas' characters are imbedded in in history; and this is precisely the new soul force we need in order to be able to follow our own stream of development backwards in this life and right on into earlier lives. It is not to be thought of as a picture that suddenly arises, nor did it for Rudolf Steiner personally, but rather like the building up of a painting by slow, steady brush strokes – after a time a clearer picture emerges. In order for this to happen, careful and hard work are required, with these fired by a driving desire to work into new realities.

The translation of particular words needs clarification:
The word "Werk" needs special attention. It may mean 'the work that we do', or 'a mechanical thing that works – a mechanism', or 'a work that we undertake – a project' , or 'action(s)'. In the second last sense, we may sometimes understand Rudolf Steiner to be indicating the 'human project' in the largest time sense.
"Bahn" I have not been able to bring satisfactorily over into English. On the one hand, it means the railway, but also possibly simply the 'way'. It could often even be translated as simply 'street', 'lane' or 'avenue'. Its more essential meaning seems to me to be what we would call something like a 'railroad or road bed' (before the iron rails are laid on it), thus really a 'prepared way'.

## Translator's Notes

"Kreis" can be interpreted as circle, circuit, orbit; but the former implies a line around a centre point, the second is usually more mundane in English: electric circuit, racing circuit, and implies the route around; the third we use for the planets, etc., as a fixed path around something. Rudolf Steiner often wants to use it in the 2nd and 3rd sense combined for the human being's path, but as a circling, spiraling route through different lives – and connected with 'will'.

"Ort" is translated as 'place' (point or standpoint), but it is often combined with other words where it may be left out. It seems to me Rudolf Steiner very definitely intended to direct us to what might be called 'spiritual places' with how he uses this word. I have tried to include it systematically whether it sounded a bit clumsy or not.

The same may be said for "Stätte" as for "Ort", but "Stätte" can be seen as a bigger place, a 'site', a place for an institution or where a large project can take place.

"voll" means simply 'full', but is often used by Rudolf Steiner in these plays in places where we would not use the word 'full' in English. Thus 'full light', 'full life', etc. For English the word must be broadened out to an appropriate concept, thus: full daylight brightness, a fully involved and active life, and so on.

"Wissen/Kenntnis" the difference between these two is not easy to bring into the translation but is of particular importance in Rudolf Steiner's works. In German, "Kenntnis" tends to indicate items of knowledge, awareness of specific units of knowledge; "Wissen" is more active, is often more like the 'knowing' after learning to do something, ie. a trade, etc.

"Frau" may be woman, wife or lady, but in German they often use both "Herr" and "Frau" in a diminutive form (thus Herr John, Frau Susan) for respected individuals who are not quite in the family and cannot be addressed as "Du", the informal 'you'. Whether Rudolf Steiner is intending this here or something else, is not entirely clear. Yet in any event, he does speak of Frau Sophia, Frau Bald and Frau Theodora in a similar way, and I have wanted to observe this in the translation.

## Page

**151**     *Lucifer*, is played by the woman who plays Helena in Scene One of **Initiation**.

         *Ahriman*, is played by a man.

**152**     *Keen*, in German 'Kuhne' – the last e is pronounced; the name may signify keen, bold; also: experienced, wise.

**153**     *unrealities*, German: 'Wesenlose'; more literally: 'what has no being or no beings in it'

**158**     *phantasmagorical game*, the German word 'Gaukelspiel' is used, which is juggling, conjuring, and trickery all rolled into one.

         *I am not*, or 'I am not it' or 'I am not that'; what is referred to is not indicated exactly.

**159**     *in the shining*, used here for the rhyme, literally: in appearances.

**160**     *a struggle for existence*, or 'one of life's battles', etc.

**164**     The reading of this last page of the scene is difficult. I read it that Capesius at first is overwhelmed by and accepts Benedictus's indications, but then after the dotted line his doubts return and he is unsure and wants to hold himself independent of Benedictus's indications if he can.

**165**     *Difficult soul ...* , there may be a double play on words here: **A** My difficult situation is driving me to get advice from you (Benedictus) ; **B** My difficult situation is now forcing me to listen, for once, to your(Benedictus) advice.

         *There should ...* , there may be a double play on words here as well: **A** There will never be a time I will not give you what you wish; **B** There should never be a time when you fail to know what you wish to have from me.

         *with horror*, or by a horror' ; see note p.**222**.

**171**     *Self-seeking*, or self-conceit, or selfishness.

**180**     *One*, all capitalized "one's" are that way in the German.

**193**     *mind*, or 'spirit'.

**195**     *Demons*, or daemons, see note p.**36**.

**196**     The Fairy Tale of the Magic Spring.

**202**     *Daemon*, or demon, see note p.**36**.

**215**     *Evil One*, or simply 'evil'.

**216**     *flaws*, literally also: 'spots' or 'stains'.

**220**     *galleries*, literally as elsewhere: 'shafts'.

## Translator's Notes

**222** *A horror*, the sense of this passage depends on whether one takes the word 'horror' in the medieval sense of a being or not. I do. Alternative translation to lines 3 + 4 might be: I am almost overwhelmed by horror … There's a crackling – oh, there's a banging about the room;

**227** *household*, literally 'your people'; presumably people in his employ and living as part of his household.

**230** *he*; 'it' might be expected, but 'he' is used in the German.

**239** The Fairy Tale of Good and Evil.

**Scene Ten**: Steiner said every word in this scene was written exactly, in order to correctly portray vision into the Akashic record.

**263** *Lord of All Desire*, literally: Commander/Ruler of Desires/Wishes.

*We*; Steiner has here "er" which refers to the masculine noun "Gebieter" = Lord, but Lucifer is definitely of a feminine nature in these dramas and 'he' does not work in English; I have therefore chosen the royal 'we' as also neutral.

*eluded your efforts*, alternatively: withdrawn herself from your work.

**264** These two lines are unclear. Another reading might be that they refer to the 'words' four lines above. Alternative translation:

They will illumine the darkness,
They will dim down the light,

*forever*, not in the German; added to complete the rhythm.

ISBN 1412023b5-3
9 781412 023658